Manual for Use of the New Dale-Chall Readability Formula

Jeanne S. Chall
Edgar Dale

Brookline Books

This manual is excerpted from *Readability Revisited: The New Dale-Chall Readability Formula*, by Jeanne S. Chall and Edgar Dale (ISBN 1-57129-008-7; Brookline Books, 1995).

ISBN 1-57129-012-5

Published by
Brookline Books
P.O. Box 1047 • Cambridge, Massachusetts 02238-1047

Contents

This manual contains the instructions for applying the New Dale-Chall Readability Formula — a method for estimating the comprehension difficulty of texts from beginning to advanced levels. The manual is based on the book *Readability Revisited: The New Dale-Chall Readability Formula*, which contains the same set of instructions for applying the formula, together with evidence of its validity. *Readability Revisited* also treats the main approaches to readability over the past 70 years (classic, cognitive-structural, and judgment)—their theoretic and research bases as well as their practical uses.

AN OVERVIEW OF READABILITY MEASUREMENT

It should be remembered that readability formulas estimate difficulty on the basis of the factors that have the highest prediction of difficulty. What makes readability measures work is that in natural language, the various factors tend to be related in a similar way to independent measures of text difficulty. Thus, when one writes simple texts—for either children or adults who have limited reading ability—one tends to write about familiar topics, using familiar words, short sentences, and simple organization.

Most of the classic readability formulas have found the strongest predictor of overall text difficulty to be word difficulty—whether measured as word frequency, familiarity, or word length. One of these factors is usually sufficient for accurate measurement, since most word factors are also related to each other (Chall, 1958; Chall & Conard, 1991; Klare, 1963 and 1984). That word length and word difficulty are highly related was demonstrated by the noted philologist George Kingsley Zipf (1935), who found that for all alphabetic languages the common, more concrete, easier words tended to be the shorter words. He further showed that when longer words are used frequently, they tend to become shorter, e.g., *television* to *TV* in the US and *telly* in Britain.

The next best predictor of comprehension difficulty in classic readability formulas is sentence length. Sentence length stands up quite well as a predictor of syntactic complexity—even better than more complex syntactic measures based on sophisticated linguistic theories. (See Bormuth, 1971, and MacGinitie & Tretiak, 1971.)

Once words and sentences are used in a readability formula, little is usually gained by adding other word and sentence factors to the formula. (See, however, the Bormuth formula, 1964, which uses two word difficulty factors: word length and unfamiliar words, according to the original Dale-Chall formula). Such word features as concreteness versus abstractness also distinguish easy from hard texts and tend to give similar results as an easy/hard vocabulary continuum. For example, the chances are great that words judged to be concrete would be on the Dale list of 3,000 words known by 4th graders. Those not on the list would generally be judged to be more abstract.

No readability formula is a complete and full measure of text difficulty. It measures only a limited number of the many characteristics that make text easy or hard to read and understand. An awareness of these limitations will lead to a wiser and more satisfactory use of readability measures. Hopefully, it will avoid a mechanical approach that can lead to disappointment.

The New Dale-Chall Formula

The new Dale-Chall formula is based on the two most potent factors in classic readability measurement: semantic (word) difficulty, and syntactic (sentence) difficulty. These two, together, correlate .92 with reading comprehension as determined by cloze comprehension scores[1].

The greater predictive power of the new formula stems from several sources: a new set of criterion passages that uses cloze procedure for estimating compre-

---

[1] In the original formula, the word and sentence factors together correlated .70 with reading comprehension.

hension difficulty, an updated word list, and improved rules for counting words as familiar or unfamiliar. Other changes in the new formula include a choice for reporting text difficulty—either as cloze scores[2] or as reading levels[3].

The new Dale-Chall formula provides guidelines for making an optimal match between texts and readers by estimating reading abilities of the intended audience, their background knowledge, motivation, purposes for reading, and the availability of assistance from teachers or knowledgeable peers. The new formula also suggests ways to make judgments about the influence of cognitive-structural factors on the reading difficulty of written text.

Guidelines are also presented in the following pages for interpreting the formula scores for use in research and practice. Sample selections from a variety of texts at different levels of difficulty are included in the Appendix to illustrate the various readablity scores.

AN OVERVIEW OF THE INSTRUCTIONS FOR USING THE NEW DALE-CHALL FORMULA

Instructions for selecting samples, for counting sentences and unfamiliar words, and for obtaining cloze and reading level scores are given on this and the following pages.

Worksheet A on page 8 is used for recording the basic data and the readability scores for each of the samples and for the entire text.

Worksheet B, page 9, contains instructions for judging reader characteristics and for recording them.

Worksheet C, page 10, contains instructions for making judgments about the cognitive-structural aspects of text and for recording them.

General Instructions

1. Enter all identifying information before the analysis.

2. *Selecting Exact 100-Word Samples.* For each sample, record the page number and note the words that begin and end the sample. To select an exact 100-word sample, begin with the first word in a sentence, and count to 100. Include any headings that fall within the sample.

- *For books of 150 pages or longer,* select one sample systematically from every 50th page, starting near the beginning, and systematically thereafter from every 50th page.
- *For books of 5 to 150 pages,* select 3 samples from the beginning, middle, and end. Do *not* use opening or closing pages, since these tend to be easier or harder than the rest of the text. If the writing style is not even, select 4 or 5 samples.
- *For selections of 4 pages or less,* select 2 samples— one near the beginning and one near the end, but not exactly the beginning or end.

3. Record the number of *complete sentences* on Worksheet A. (See p. 3 for specific instructions).

4. Record the number of *unfamiliar words* on Worksheet A. (See more specific instructions on pp. 3-5).

5. Obtain the *Cloze Score* (see Table 1, pp. 21-28) by reading the number of unfamiliar words (on the left) and the number of sentences (on top). Record the score for each sample on Worksheet A.

6. Obtain the *Reading Level* (see Table 2, pp. 29-35) by reading the number of unfamiliar words (on the left) and the number of sentences (on top). Record the level for each sample on Worksheet A.

Repeat for each sample, then obtain *Average Cloze Scores* and *Reading Levels*. Record on Worksheet A.

7. Judge and record reader characteristics (Worksheet B).

8. Judge and record the cognitive and structural aspects of text (Worksheet C).

Shorter Samples

For samples shorter than 100 words, e.g., test items or brief instructions:

Turn the number of sentences into a percentage — that is, prorate to 100 words. Use the following formula:

$$\frac{sentences}{words\ in\ selection} = \begin{array}{l} number\ of\ sentences \\ in\ 100\ word\ sample \end{array}$$

Example: A sample of 60 words and 3 sentences converts to 5 sentences per 100 words.

Turn the number of unfamiliar words into a percentage — that is, prorate to 100 words. Use the following formula:

$$\frac{unfamiliar\ words}{words\ in\ selection} = \begin{array}{l} number\ of\ unfamiliar\ words \\ in\ 100\text{-}word\ sample \end{array}$$

Example: A sample of 60 words with 5 unfamiliar words converts to 8 unfamiliar words per 100 words.

Use the tables on pages 21-35 to obtain Cloze and/or Reading Level scores.

---

[2] Cloze scores are the number of correct inserts out of 100 deleted words. The higher the cloze scores, the easier the text.

[3] Reading levels are the approximate reading ability levels for reading and understanding the text. The higher the reading level, the harder the text.

Assessing Several Aspects of Readability

The new Dale-Chall readability scores are to be recorded on Worksheet A.

To broaden the overall judgment of optimal difficulty for readers of given reading ability, background knowledge and purpose, Worksheets B and C are suggested.

To obtain a more complete view of the match between the reader and the text, all three Worksheets should be examined.

SPECIFIC INSTRUCTIONS FOR USING THE NEW DALE-CHALL READABILITY FORMULA

1. *Counting the Number of Words in a Sample*

Words commonly considered words are to be counted as such.

a. *Count the following as one word*:

- Hyphenated words and contractions
  Example: *lady-in-waiting* is counted as one word.
  don't is one word.
  (Do not include words hyphenated because of syntax. Thus, words like *task-relevant* and *anxiety-provoking* are counted as two words each.)

- Numerals
  Example: *10* is one word.
  1978 is one word.
  1,000,000 is one word.

- Compound names of persons and places
  Example: *St. John* is one word.
  Van Buren is one word.
  del Rio is one word.
  (However, *New York* and *New England* are counted as two words each.)

- Initials in names of persons are part of the surname.
  Example: *Elizabeth B. Browning* counts as two words.
  T. S. Eliot counts as one word.

- Abbreviations, initials, and acronyms
  Example: *Y.W.C.A.* is counted as one word.
  A.M. and *P.M.* count as one word each.
  J.F.K. is counted as one word.
  NOW is counted as one word.

b. *Count the following as separate words*:

- Each word in the name of an organization, law, or title
  Example: *Declaration of Independence* is counted as three words.
  American Automobile Association is three words.
  A Tale of Two Cities is counted as five words.

- Each word in place names
  Example: *Empire State Building* is counted as three words.
  Twenty-third Avenue is counted as two words
  McDonald's Restaurant is counted as two words.
  Miller's Pond is counted as two words.

2. *Count the Number of Sentences*:

For exact 100-word samples, count *only* the number of complete sentences.

- Count as complete sentences those that end in a period, question, or exclamation mark. (Semi-colons and colons are not considered to be sentence breaking markers.)

- Topic headings are counted as sentences, even when they contain no punctuation or contain only one word.

3. *Count the Unfamiliar Words*:

Underline all unfamiliar words as many times as they appear, except for "unfamiliar" names and places. Unfamiliar names and places are counted only once in a sample.

a. *Count the following as familiar words*:

- All words on the new Dale List of 3,000 words, including variations noted in parentheses.

- Regular plurals and possessives of words on the list (-'s, -s, -es, -ies).
  Example: *boy's* is familiar because *boy* is on the list.
  girls is familiar because *girl* is on the list.
  churches is familiar because *church* is on the list.
  armies is familiar because *army* is on the list.
  Note: *Irregular plurals*, if *not* on the list or in parentheses, are counted *unfamiliar*.

A SPECIAL NOTE ON COUNTING UNFAMILIAR WORDS:
It is well to remember that words *on* the list of 3,000 words are known to 80 percent of students in 4th grade. These words may be viewed as the most elemental words in the English language — words about home, family, food, clothing, emotions, etc. Generally, these words and their meanings are known without formal schooling. Most words *not* on the list can be thought of as "educated" words, those usually learned in school from about 4th grade on, and primarily from reading. Usually these are specialized, technical, abstract, or literary words.

We suggest that the analyst make a first approximation as to whether a word is familiar ("elemental") or unfamiliar ("educated"). The list (and guidelines) should then be consulted to confirm the analyst's judgment. With practice this procedure becomes quite rapid.

Example: *oxen* is unfamiliar even though *ox* is on the list (irregular plural).

• Words on the list with the following endings:

-d, -ed, -ied. Examples:
　voted is familiar because *vote* is on the list.
　tripped is familiar because *trip* is on the list.
　carried is familiar because *carry* is on the list.

-ing. Examples:
　doing is familiar because *do* is on the list.
　dropping is familiar because *drop* is on the list.

-s, -es, -ies. Examples:
　works is familiar because *work* is on the list.
　guesses is familiar because *guess* is on the list.
　worries is familiar because *worry* is on the list.

-r, -er, -est, -ier, -iest. Examples:
　dancer is familiar because *dance* is on the list.
　longer is familiar because *long* is on the list.
　bravest is familiar because *brave* is on the list.
　prettier is familiar because *pretty* is on the list.
　happiest is familiar because *happy* is on the list.

Note: Count a word unfamiliar if two or more endings are added to a word on the list, e.g., *clippings* (*-ing* + *-s*).

• Compound and hyphenated words on the list are counted familiar if both components are on the list. (They are counted *unfamiliar* if one or both components are *not* on the list.)
Example: *firelight* is considered familiar because *fire* and *light* are listed.

b. *Count the following as unfamiliar words:*

• Words not on the list.

• Words on the list with the following endings: *-tion, -ation, -ment, -ly, -y.*

• Hyphenated and compound words that are not on the list or if one or both components are not listed.
Example: *will-of-the-wisp* is counted as one unfamiliar word, since *wisp* is not on the list.
　work-oriented is counted as one unfamiliar word, since *work* is on the list but *orient* is not.
(Count as two unfamiliar words if both are not on the list.)

• Proper names and places not on the list. *But count unfamiliar only once in a 100-word sample.*

Guidelines for Numerals

The formula is not intended to measure the readability of texts whose content is primarily mathematical. However, for texts with occasional use of numbers, the following guidelines[4] are suggested.

i. Count as familiar the following:

• Numerical quantities having 5 or fewer digits
Example: *28,309* is counted familiar.
　1,000,000 is counted unfamiliar.

• The signs: =, +, -, x, ÷

• Numbers used to express monetary values when they contain three or fewer digits to the left of the decimal point.
Example: *$127.00* is counted familiar.
　$234.56 is counted familiar.
　$1,420.00 is counted unfamiliar.
　$34,125.45 is counted unfamiliar.

• Ordinal numbers with one or two digits ending in *-st* and *-nd*

---

[4] These guidelines are adapted, with the generous permission of the author, the late Dr. Ted K. Kilty, who tested these mathematical terms on children in the fourth grade. For the complete research, see Kilty, Ted K., *The Readability of Numerical Quantities and Abbreviations,* Western Michigan University Center for Educational Studies, 1979.

Example: *1st* is counted as familiar.
            92nd is counted as familiar.
But: *139th* is counted as unfamiliar.
            2,003rd is counted as unfamiliar.

- The abbreviations: *yd., ft., in., gal.*

ii. Count as unfamiliar:

- Time, when written in more than one numeral. Example: *12:15 o'clock* is counted unfamiliar (*o'clock* is familiar).

- All Roman numerals.

- All decimals, except when used to express monetary values as above.

- All fractions.

The words and symbols for percent (%, per cent, and percent) are each counted as one unfamiliar word.

Reminder: Repetitions of Unfamiliar Words

- The following are counted as often as they are used: Dates, e.g., June 5, 1962, are unfamiliar. The unfamiliar words in organizations. The unfamiliar words in titles of books, documents, films, etc. Abbreviations and acronyms.

- "Unfamiliar" names and places are to be counted unfamiliar *only once* in each sample.

Uses of the New Dale-Chall Readability Formula

For What Kinds of Texts is the New Formula Suitable?

The new Dale-Chall formula is appropriate for use with connected texts including articles and books—fiction and non-fiction. Most books in science, social studies, literature and the humanities can be appropriately assessed. The formula is also appropriate for analyses of articles in newspapers and magazines, and technical reports.

In general, technical materials in mathematics that contain many numbers, symbols, and equations are not as well served by the formula. Some poetry is also less well assessed by the new Dale-Chall formula and by most classic readability measures. Because the metaphorical language in much poetry uses familiar words in rare or figurative senses, the readability scores obtained often underestimate true difficulty.

The new formula can be used to rate passages at reading levels 1 to college graduate level. (The original formula rated passages only at reading levels 4 and above). The lower ratings were made possible by the Bormuth criterion passages, which included selections below the 4th reading level. With extrapolation, the new formula also discriminates between reading levels 1, 2 and 3. The degree of confidence, however, is not as great as it is for reading levels 4 through 16.

What Factors Besides Word and Sentence Difficulty Should Be Assessed?

The new Dale-Chall readability estimates are enhanced by judgments about other factors which are known to be associated with readability, but are not directly measured by the formula. These are noted below, in the instructions, and on the worksheets. We suggest these qualitative judgments be taken into account when making an appropriate match between readers and text. Indeed, if the text is favorable on these qualities, it may actually be less difficult than the readability score estimates. If the text is low on these qualities, it may be more difficult to read than the formula estimates.

- Unfamiliar and technical words are used well in context and/or are clearly defined in the text, in footnotes, or in glossaries.
- Unfamiliar concepts are explained in terms of the reader's previous knowledge.
- Chapters, sections, and the entire book are well organized, with use of headings, questions, and other aids to improve structure.
- Questions are inserted in the text preceding, within, or following teaching units.
- Illustrations to explain difficult ideas are placed close to the text they amplify and contain helpful captions.

These are to be "checked off" as characteristics of the text, with an indication of the degree to which they are found in the text.

It should be noted that these qualitative characteristics enhance comprehension and retention in textbooks and instructional materials, particularly at levels 4 and above. Further, these may not be reflected in the two factors in the new Dale-Chall formula. Hence, their consideration adds another dimension to the readability scores. They are not substitutes for the readability scores. They are a supplement to them.

Matching Texts to Readers

The purpose of readability assessment is to effect a "best match" between intended readers and texts. A readability formula is a tool for predicting the difficulty of text. It tells how hard the material probably is in terms of relative difficulty or in relation to the reading ability of prospective readers. But it does not tell how hard it should be. For that, it helps to know the reading abilities of the prospective readers, their background knowledge with regard to the content of the text, and the purpose of the material's use (whether it will be supplemented by a teacher's instruction or whether it is to be read independently).

Information on the intended readers might include, when available, their reading ability, their previous knowledge and interest in the topic, and how the material is to be read—whether independently or as part of instruction.

For students, reading ability may be estimated by scores or bands on a recently administered reading test.[5] If these are not available, estimates of reading ability may be made by noting the readability of the books, magazines, and newspaper they read. For adults, the last school grade reached may be used as an estimate of reading ability, although it may be higher than that found when tests are used.[6]

When the topics of texts are familiar to the intended readers, and when readers find them of interest, they will usually be easier to read. Unfamiliar texts and those less interesting will generally be harder to read. Also, the same texts read with assistance from a teacher or knowledgeable peers are easier to read than when read without help.

Thus, optimal difficulty comes from an interaction between the text, the reader, and his or her purpose in reading. Generally, most readability researchers have considered an optimal match for independent reading to be on a level that matches the reader's ability.

Recent research indicates, however, that when used for instructional purposes, the text may be somewhat above the student's level to encourage optimal development of reading comprehension among children and adults who are learning to read. (See Chall, Conard & Harris, 1977; Chall, Jacobs & Baldwin, 1990; Chall & Conard, 1991a.) Vygotsky, 1978, proposed that optimal difficulty for learning be at a level of "proximal development" for learners—i.e., above their level of development, not below,

when assisted by a teacher or more knowledgeable peers. For elementary and high school students, reading achievement improves when the books used for instruction (with teacher and/or peer assistance) are challenging—i.e., somewhat above their reading levels, not lower.

It would appear, then, that instructional materials, particularly those from which students receive instruction, need to be sufficiently challenging to produce optimal, long-term growth in reading. This is particularly true when teachers can give assistance with background knowledge, new vocabulary, and the kind of thinking required.

The new Dale-Chall readability scores, as well as those from most classic formulas, can be viewed as predicting the level suitable for independent reading, since the passages were tested during independent silent reading, without teachers' instruction or assistance. However, if the text is to be used for instruction—i.e., students receive help from a teacher—the optimal text readability could be harder than the students' tested reading level.

Materials to be read by the general public, e.g., patent medicine inserts, instructions for filing income tax, instructions for using household machinery, on the other hand, should be as easy as possible to convey accurate information to most of the adult population, even those with limited reading ability.

Textbooks generally serve the purpose of developing the students' knowledge in a particular field as well as enhancing their language and reading ability. Therefore, when used with instruction and guidance from teachers and/or more advanced peers, they may be on a level that is somewhat above students' tested reading ability. (See Chall et al., 1977; Chall & Conard, 1991; Chall, Jacobs & Baldwin, 1990; Hayes, Wolfer & Wolfe, 1993.)[7]

Optimal Difficulty for Listening as Compared to Reading

Generally, the Dale-Chall formula can also be used to estimate listening comprehension difficulty. When selections are placed in order of increasing difficulty for listening comprehension, the ranks will tend to be the same as for reading comprehension. However, they tend to differ

---

[5] There has been much discussion about the meaning and validity of the "exact" grade level scores (e.g., 3.8, 7.4) on standardized reading tests. Nearly all test publishers now report individual scores as a band, or range, as is done in both the original and new Dale-Chall readability formulas. It is therefore suggested that the band or range be used.

[6] Before "automatic" or "age level promotions" became standard practice (about 40 to 50 years ago), the last school grade reached was a reasonable estimate of reading ability. It still is quite useful. Because many unskilled readers are promoted, however, the reading levels of adolescents and adults may be lower than their last grade reached.

[7] There has been a preference for "easier" texts from the early 1920s and many researchers and teachers still prefer easier texts. However, our research (noted above) and that of Hayes and his associates indicate that when more challenging materials are used for instruction, over many years, students achieve higher scores in reading and language development than those using less challenging materials.

This is particularly true for books at a 4th grade level and higher which contain ever more difficult, abstract and technical words, and more difficult concepts. Thus reading with an instructor, at a level beyond that of the student's present development (his or her reading level, or Vygotsky's level of proximal development), the student has a better chance of learning more difficult concepts and more difficult words—the strongest factors in reading achievement and reading comprehension difficulty. Using books that are on the student's present level orbelow, helps in the development of fluency and rate, but not as much in reading comprehension.

for levels. For example, for listening comprehension, texts at reading levels 8 and below will usually be easier to understand when heard than when read. This is because spoken language develops faster than written language until about 8th grade. For levels at about 8th to 12th grade, texts will be of about equal difficulty when heard as when read. Beyond a 12th grade level, the same text may be harder to understand when heard than when read (Chall, 1983; Sticht, Beck, Hauke, Kleiman & James, 1974).

Judgments of Cognitive & Structural Features

Readability estimates are enhanced by taking into account cognitive and structural factors known to be associated with readability, but which are not directly measured by readability formulas. If the text has good organization and explains ideas well, it may be less difficult than the readability formula estimates. If the text is weak on these qualities, it may be more difficult to read than the formula suggests. Estimates of organization and idea difficulty are not substitutes for readability scores. They are supplements to them. (See Worksheet C.)

Use of Formulas for Writing and Editing

Readability formulas have also been used by writers, editors, and publishers to write, rewrite, and revise reading materials to specified readability levels. This has been criticized because the lowering of readability scores has not always produced better comprehension and it has also been reported to lead to more ambiguous writing (see Davison & Kantor, 1980). Indeed, the early developers of readability formulas cautioned against the use of readability formulas as rules for writing or rewriting (Horn, 1930). Readability formulas are valid, they claimed, for predicting reading difficulty, but they are too limited when used as rules for writing.

Readability *principles*, rather than readability measures, can be helpful in revising and writing materials for readers of specified reading levels. An analogy with reading tests is useful here, since readability measurements are in many ways similar to standardized reading tests. Readability measures assess the difficulty of reading material as a standardized reading test measures the reading ability of students. Similar to standardized reading tests, readability measures deal only with samples of the text and important aspects of difficulty, not with all aspects of it. Therefore, it is also necessary to look further to the cognitive-structural features of the text. Scores from readability measures, like scores from standardized reading tests, are based on only the most potent predictors of reading difficulty. Since both readability formulas and reading tests measure only limited aspects of readability and reading ability, judgment is needed for full interpretation. Also, to effect a change in true readability or reading ability, more than the few factors measured need to be modified.

It has therefore been common among readability researchers to call for caution in the use of readability formulas to guide writing and editing. From the early years of readability research, rewriting to desired readability standards was viewed in terms of using guidelines and helpful techniques, rather than changing words and sentences to obtain lower scores (Dale & Hager, 1950; Flesch, 1949; Gunning, 1952, 1968). A readability formula is suggested for assessing a manuscript and for sensitizing writers to the factors of difficulty. The writing and rewriting for greater readability are usually presented in qualitative terms of organization, conceptual difficulty, defining of technical and difficult words, and the like.

Generally the most effective revisions in terms of improved comprehension were those that changed the organizational structure, the appeal, and other qualitative aspects in addition to the vocabulary and sentence structure (see Klare, 1984, for a sensitive analysis of the uses of readability formulas for writing, and also an earlier review of the research by Chall, 1958).

REFERENCES

Bormuth, J.R. (1964). Readability: A new approach. *Reading Research Quarterly, 1*, pp. 79-132.

Bormuth, J.R. (1971). *Development of standards of readability: Report of development* (Project No. 9-0237). Chicago: University of Chicago. (ERIC Document Reproduction Service No. ED 054-233).

Chall, J.S. (1958; reprinted, 1974). *Readability: An appraisal of research and application.* Bureau of Educational Research Monographs, No. 34. Columbus, OH: Ohio State University Press. Reprinted (1974) by Bowker Publishing Co., Ltd., Epping, Essex, England.

Chall, J.S. (1983). *Stages of reading development.* New York: McGraw-Hill.

Chall, J.S. (1995). *Readability revisited: The new Dale-Chall readability formula.* Cambridge, MA: Brookline Books.

Chall, J.S., & Conard, S.S. (1991). *Should textbooks challenge students? The case for easier or harder books.* New York: Teachers College Press.

Chall, J.S., Conard, S., & Harris, S. (1977). *An analysis of textbooks in relation to declining SAT scores.* Princeton, NJ: Educational Testing Service and the College Entrance Examination Board.

Chall, J.S., Jacobs, V.A., & Baldwin, L.E. (1990). *The reading crisis: Why poor children fall behind.* Cambridge, MA: Harvard University Press.

Dale, E., & Hager, H. (1950). *Some suggestions for writing health materials.* New York: National Tuberculosis Association.

Davison, A., & Kantor, R.N. (1982). On the failure of readability formulas to define readable texts: A case study from adoptions. *Reading Research Quarterly, 17*, pp. 187-209.

Flesch, R. (1949 & 1974). *The art of readable writing: With the Flesch readability formula.* New York: Harper & Row.

Gunning, R. (1952, 1968). *The technique of clear writing.* New York: McGraw-Hill.

Hayes, D., Wolfer, L., & Wolfe, M. (1993). *Was the decline in SAT scores caused by simplified school texts?* Paper presented at the Annual Meeting of the American Sociological Association, Miami, FL.

Horn, E. (1937). *Methods of instruction in the social studies.* New York: Charles Scribner's Sons.

Klare, G.R. (1963). *The measurement of readability.* Ames, IA: Iowa State University Press.

Klare, G.R. (1984). Readability. In P. D. Pearson (Ed.), *Handbook of reading research.* New York: Longman, pp. 681-744.

MacGinitie, W., & Tretiak, R. (1971). Sentence depth measures as predictors of reading difficulty. *Reading Research Quarterly, 6*, pp. 364-376.

Sticht, T.G., Beck, L.J., Hauke, R.N., Kleiman, G.M., & James, J.H. (1974). *Auding and reading.* Alexandria, VA: Human Resources Research Organization.

THE NEW DALE-CHALL READABILITY FORMULA
Worksheet A

1.

Book or Article _____

Source _____

Publisher _____

Date of Publication _____

Analyzed by _____

Date of Analysis_____

		2		3	4	5	6
	Page Number	From	To	Number of Sentences	Number of Unfamiliar Words	Cloze Score (From Table 2-1)	Reading Level (From Table 2-2)
Sample 1							
Sample 2							
Sample 3							
Sample 4							
Sample 5							
Sample 6							
Sample 7							
Sample 8							
						Average of Cloze Scores	Average Reading Level

THE NEW DALE-CHALL READABILITY FORMULA
Worksheet B
Judging Reader Characteristics

After applying the new Dale-Chall readability formula, make an assessment of the reading abilities of the intended readers.

For assessing reading abilities, use the reading levels from a reading achievement test, last school grade achieved, or the estimated level of books or magazines that are read by the prospective readers. Make an educated guess if objective data are not available.

In general, if the material is to be read independently, it should be at or below the readers' reading level. If the material is to be used for instructional purposes aided by teacher instruction, it can be on the readers' level or on a higher level.

Approximate Average Reading Level _____   Range _____

How were reading levels determined?   _____ by tests   _____ estimated

How is the material to be used? Check one or more:

_____ For independent reading

_____ For instruction, with little teacher assistance

_____ For instruction, with much teacher assistance

Are prospective readers likely to be interested in the topic?   _____ yes   _____ no

Comments _____

_____

_____

Are they likely to be interested in the way the topic is presented?   _____ yes   _____ no

Comments _____

_____

_____

THE NEW DALE-CHALL READABILITY FORMULA
Worksheet C
Judging Cognitive-Structural Aspects of Text

Estimate whether the text organization, its conceptual difficulty and density, and its format may make the text more difficult, less difficult, or about the same as that predicted by the new Dale-Chall Readability Formula.

For each of the following characteristics, the analyst is to judge whether it probably raises, lowers, or leaves unchanged the readability estimates obtained from the formula.

Compared with the new Dale-Chall readability scores, check the following:

	Less readable	More readable	About the same
The **prior knowledge** expected of the reader seems to make the text	_____	_____	_____

(For example, consider the following: Does the text require more or less background knowledge than assumed by the author of the text? Is much of the new information unexplained, requiring that readers already know much of what is stated, or can they make the needed inferences?)

The **vocabulary and concepts** used in the text seem to make the text	_____	_____	_____

(For example, are the unfamiliar concepts and words in the text defined, explained, and used in a rich context that will enhance its readability for the intended reader?)

The **overall organization** seems to make the text	_____	_____	_____

(For example, is the text clearly organized? Do the ideas follow logically from one another?)

The use of **headings, questions, illustrations** and **physical features** seem to make the text	_____	_____	_____

(For example, do the headings and other physical features highlight important information for the reader? Are questions used in a manner that helps the reader remember what is read? Do the illustrations help explain new and difficult ideas? Are the captions meaningful? Are the illustrations placed near the text they are to illustrate?)

A LIST OF 3,000 WORDS KNOWN BY STUDENTS IN GRADE 4

Compiled by Edgar Dale

(Revised 1983)

Consider as known words on the list with endings indicated in parentheses and words with the following endings, even though they are not noted in parentheses:

-'s, -s, -es, -ies; -d, -ed, -ied, -ing; -r, -er, -est, -ier, -iest

(For further instructions, see pages 00-00.)

A
able
aboard
about
above
absent
accept
accident
account
ache
acid
acorn
across
act
action
add
addition
address
adjust (ment)
admire
admission
adore
adult
adventure
advice
afraid
after
afternoon
afterward (s)
again
against
age
ago
agree
ah
ahead
aid
aim
air (y)
airline
airplane
airport

alarm
album
alike
alive
all
alley
alligator
all right
almost
alone
along
alongside
aloud
alphabet
already
also
always
am
A.M.
amaze (ment)
America (n)
among
amount
an
and
angel
anger
angry
animal
ankle
announce (ment)
another
answer
ant
any
anybody
anyhow
anyone
anything
anyway
anywhere
apart

apartment
ape
apiece
appear
applause
apple
April
apron
are (n't)
area (place)
arise
arithmetic
arm
army
around
arrange
arrest
arrive
arrow
arrowhead
art
artist
as
ash
aside
ask
asleep
astronaut
at
ate
atlas
attack
attend
attention
August
aunt
author
auto
automobile
autumn
avenue
awake (n)

award
away
awful
awhile
ax(e)

B
baa
baby
baby-sitter
back
backache
background
backtrack
backward(s)
bacon
bad
badge
bag
baggage
bait
bake
bakery
balance
ball
balloon
ballpoint
banana
band
bandage
bang
banjo
bank
bar
barbecue (sauce)
barber
bare
barefoot
bark
barn
barrel
base

baseball
basement
basket
basketball
bat
bath (e)
bathroom
battle
be
beach
bead
beak
beam
bean
bear
beard
beast
beat
beautiful
beauty
beaver
because
become (came)
bed
bedroom
bedspread
bee
beef
beefsteak
been
beer
beet
before
beg
beggar
begin (gan) (gun)
behave
behind
belief
believe
bell
belly

belong (ings)
below
belt
bench
bend (t)
beneath
berry
beside(s)
best
bet
better
between
beyond
bib
bible
bicycle
big (ness)
bill
billfold
billion
billy goat
bingo
bird
birth
birthday
biscuit
bit
bite
bitter
black (ness)
blackboard
blacksmith
blame
blank
blanket
blast
blastoff
blaze
bleed
bless
blew
blind

blindfold	brave (ry)	butterfly	castle	chirp	colt
blink	bread	butterscotch	cat	chocolate	column
blinker	break	button	catch	choice	comb
block	breakfast	buy	caterpillar	choke	come
blond (e)	breast	buzz	catsup	choose	comfort (able)
blood	breath (e)	by	cattle	chop	comic
bloodhound	breeze	bye	caught	chop suey	comma
bloodstream	brick		cause	chorus	command
bloom	bride	**C**	cave	chose (n)	commercial
blossom	bridge	cab	ceiling	Christmas	company
blot	bright (en)	cabbage	celebrate (ion)	church	complete
blouse	bring	cabin	cell	churn	computer
blow	broad	cage	cellar	cigarette	concrete
blue	broadcast	cake	cent	circle	conductor
blueberry	broke (n)	calendar	center	circus	cone
blush	broken-hearted	calf	cereal	citizen	connect
board	brook	call	certain	city	contest
boat	broom	came	chain	clap	continue
bobwhite	brother	camel	chair	class	control
body	brought	camera	chalk (board)	classroom	cook
bodyguard	brown	camp	champion	claw	cooky (ie)
boil	brownie	can ('t)	chance	clay	cool
bold	brush	canal	change	clean	copy
bolt	bubble	canary	channel (TV)	cleanser	cord
bomb	bucket	candle	chapter	clear	cork
bone	buckle	candy	charge	clerk	corn
bonnet	bud	cane	charm	clever	corner
boo	budge	cannon	chart	click	cornmeal
book	buffalo	cannot	chase	climate	correct
boom	bug	canoe	chatter	climb	cost
boot	buggy	canyon	cheap	clip	cottage
born	build (ing)	cap	cheat	clock	cotton
borrow	bulb	cape	check	close	couch
boss	bull	capital	checkers	closet	cough
both	bullet	capsule	checkup	cloth	could (n't)
bother	bulletin board	captain	cheek	cloud (y)	count
bottle	bumblebee	capture	cheer (ful) (ly)	clown	counter
bottom	bump (y)	car	cheese	club	country
bought	bun	card	cheeseburger	clubhouse	course
boulder	bunch	cardboard	cherry	coach	court
bounce	bundle	care	chest	coal	cousin
bow	bunk	careful (ly)	chestnut	coast	cover
bowl	bunny	careless	chew	Coast Guard	cow
bow-wow	burglar	carload	chick	coat	coward
box	burn (t)	carpenter	chicken	cob	cowboy
boxcar	burro	carpet	chief	cobweb	cozy (sy)
boy	burst	carriage	child (ren)	cocktail	crab
brace	bury	carrot	childhood	cocoa	crack
bracelet	bus	carry	chili	coconut	cracker
brain	bush	cart	chill (y)	coffee	cradle
brake	bushel	cartoon	chimney	coin	cranberry
bran	business	carve	chimpanzee	cold	crank
branch	busy	case	chin	collar	crash
brand	but	cash	china	collect (ion) (or)	crawl
brand-new	butcher	cashier	chip	college	crayon
brass	butter	cash register	chipmunk	color (ful)	crazy

cream (y)	dawn	disgrace (ful)	dump	Eskimo	far
creature	day	dish	during	evaporate	faraway
creek	daylight	dismiss	dust (y)	even	fare
creep	daytime	distance	dying	evening	farm
crib	dead	ditch		ever	farmer
cricket	deaf	dive	**E**	everlasting	far-off
crime	deal	divide	each	every	farther
cripple	dear	do	eager	everybody	fashion
crisp	death	dock	eagle	everyday	fast
croak	December	doctor	ear	everyone	fasten
crook	decide	dodge	earache	everything	fat
crop	deck	does (n't)	eardrum	everywhere	father
cross	deep	dog	early	evil	fault
crosswalk	deer	doll (y)	earn (ings)	exactly	favor
crossways	defend	dollar	earth	example	favorite
crow	delighted	done	earthquake	excellent	fear
crowd	deliver (y)	donkey	east (ern)	except	feast
crown	den	don't	Easter	exchange	feather
cruel	dentist	door	easy	excited	February
crumb	depend	doorstep	eat (en)	exciting	fed
crumble	deposit	dope	edge	excuse	feed
crush	describe	dot	education	exercise	feel
crutch	desert	double	egg	exit	feet
crust	design	dove	eight	expect	fell
cry	desire	down	eighteen	experiment	fellow
cub	desk	downstairs	eighth	explain	felt
cup (ful)	destroy	downtown	eighty	explode	female
cupboard	detective	downward (s)	either	explore	fence
cure	detergent	dozen	elastic	explosive	fern
curl (y)	devil	drag	elbow	express (way)	festival
curtain	dew	dragon	election	extra	fever
curve	dial	drain	electric	eye	few
cushion	diamond	drank	electricity	eyeball	fib
customer	dice	draw	elephant	eyebrow	fiddle
cut	dictionary	dream	elevator	eyeglass	field
cute	did (n't)	dress	eleven	eyelash	fifteen
	die	drew	elf	eyelid	fifth
D	diet	drill	elm	eyesight	fifty
dad (dy)	difference (ent)	drink	else		fig
daddy-long-legs	difficult (y)	drip	empty	**F**	fight
daily	dig	drive	encyclopedia	fable	figure
dairy	dim	driveway	end	face	file
daisy	dime	drop	endless	fact	fill
dam	dimple	drove	enemy	factory	film
damage	dine	drown	engine	fade	final
damp	ding-dong	drowsy	engineer	fail (ure)	finally
dance	dinner	drug	English	faint	find
dandy	dinosaur	drugstore	enjoy (ment)	fair	fine
danger (ous)	dip	drum	enough	fairy (land)	finger (nail) (tip)
dare	direct	drunk	enter	faith	fingerprint
dark (ness)	direction	dry	envelope	fake	finish
darling	dirt (y)	duck (ling)	equal	fall	fire
dart	disagree	due	equator	false	fireplace
dash	disappear	dug	erase	family	fire extinguisher
date	discover	dull	errand	fan	firefly
daughter	disease	dumb	escape	fancy	fire plug

fireproof	fort	gay	grandson	hamster	hid (den)
fireworks	fortune	geese	grandstand	hand (ful)	hide
first	forty	general	grape	handkerchief	hide-and-seek
fish	forward	gentle	grapefruit	handle	hideout
fist	fought	gentleman (men)	grass	handmade	hi-fi
fit	found	geography	grasshopper	handsome	high
five	fountain	get	grave	handwriting	high school
fix	four	ghost	gravel	hang	highway
fizz	fourteen	giant	graveyard	happen	hike
flag	fourth	gift	gravy	happiness	hill (y)
flame	fox	giggle	gray (grey)	happy	him
flap	frame	gill	graze	harbor	himself
flare	freckles	giraffe	grease (y)	hard	hint
flash	free	girl	great	hardware	hip
flashlight	freedom	give (n)	greedy	harm (less) (ful)	hippo
flat	freeze	glad (ness)	green	harness	hire
flavor	freight	glance	greens	harp	his
flea	fresh	glare	greet	harvest	history
flesh	Friday	glass	grew	has (n't)	hit
flew	friend	glassware	greyhound	hat	hitch
flies	friendship	glide	grill	hatch	hive
flight	frighten	globe	grin	hatchet	ho
flip	frog	glory	grind	hate	hobble
float	from	glove	grip	haul	hobby
flock	front	glow	grizzly	have (n't)	hockey
flood	frost	glue	groan	hawk	hoe
floor	frown	go	grocery	hay	hold
flour	froze	goal	groom	he	holdup
flow	fruit	goat	ground	head	hole
flower	fry	gobble	group	headache	holiday
flu	fudge	God (g)	grow (n)	headline	hollow
flunk	fuel	godmother	growl	headquarters	holster
flute	full	gold (en)	grown-up	heal	holy
fly	fun	goldfish	growth	health (y)	home
foam	funny	golf	guard	heap	home run
fog (gy)	fur	gone	guess	hear	homesick
fold	furniture	good	guest	heard	homework
folks	further	good-by (bye)	guide	heart	honest
follow		goodies	guitar	heat	honey
fond	**G**	goodness	gum	heaven	honeybee
food	gallon	goose	gun	heavy	honk
fool (ish)	gallop	got (gotten)	guy	heel	honor
foot	gamble	government	gym	height	hood
football	game	governor		held	hoof
footpath	gang	gown	**H**	helicopter	hook
footprint	gangster	grab	habit	hell	hoot
footsteps	garage	grace	had (n't)	he'll	hop
for	garbage	grade	hail	hello	hope
force	garden	grain	hair (y)	helmet	hopscotch
forehead	gargle	grand	half	help (ful)	horn
forest	gas	grandchild	hall	hen	horse
forever	gasoline	granddaughter	Halloween	her	hose
forget (ful)	gate	grandfather	hallway	herd	hospital
forgot (ten)	gather	grandma	ham	here	hot
fork	gauge	grandmother	hamburger	hero	hot dog
form	gave	grandpa	hammer	herself	hotel

hound	into	key	leather	London	mark
hour	introduce	kick	leave	lone	market
house	invent (or)	kid	led	lonesome	marriage
housekeeper	invite	kidnap	left	long	marry
housewife	iron	kill	leg	look	marvelous
how	is (n't)	kind (ness)	lemon (ade)	loop	mash
howl	island	kindergarten	lend	loose	mask
hug	It ('ll) ('s)	king	length	lord (L)	master
huge	I've	kiss	lens	lose	match
hum	ivory	kit	leopard	loss	mate
human	ivy	kitchen	less	lost	matter
hump		kite	lesson	lot	mattress
hundred	**J**	kitten	let	lotion	may
hung	jack	kitty	letter	loud	May
hunger	jack-o-lantern	knee	lettuce	loudspeaker	maybe
hungry	jacket	kneel	level	love	mayor
hunk	jackpot	knew	liar	low	me
hunt	jacks	knife (ves)	liberty	luck (y)	meadow
hurricane	jail	knight	librarian	luggage	meal
hurry	jam	knit	library	lullaby	mean
hurt	janitor	knob	lick	lumber	meaning
husband	January	knock	lid	lump	measure
hush	jar	knot	lie	lunch	meat
hut	jaw	know (n)	life	lung	medicine
hymn	jawbone		lifeboat	luxury	meet
	jay		lifeguard	lying	melon
I	jaywalker	**L**	life preserver		melt
I	jazz	lace	lift	**M**	member
ice (y)	jeans	lad	light (ness)	ma	memorize
iceberg	jeep	ladder	lighthouse	macaroni	memory
ice cream	jelly	lady	lightning	machine	men
I'd	jerk	laid	like	mad	mend
idea	jet	lake	lily	made	mention
if	jewel (ry)	lamb	limb	magazine	menu
igloo	jig	lame	lime	magic	meow
ill	job	lamp	Lincoln, Abraham	magnet	merchant
I'll	join	land	line	maid	mermaid
I'm	joke	lane	linen	mail	merry
imagine	jolly	language	lion	mailman	merry-go-round
important	journey	lantern	lip	major	mess
impossible	joy (ful)	lap	lipstick	majorette	message
improve	judge	large	liquor	make	messenger
in	jug	last	list	make-believe	met
inch	juice (y)	late	listen	male	metal
indeed	July	laugh	litterbug	mama	meter
Indian	jump	laundry	little	man	mice
indoors	June	law	live	manage	microphone
industry	jungle	lawn	liver	manager	middle
ink	junk	lawyer	lizard	mane	midget
inn	just	lay	load	manners	midnight
insect		lazy	loaf (ves)	many	midsummer
inside	**K**	lead	loan	map	might (y)
inspection	kangaroo	leaf (ves)	lobster	maple	mile
instead	ketchup	leak	lock	marble	milk
intend	keep (kept)	lean	log	march	milkshake
interest	kettle	leap	lollipop	March	mill

million	move (able)	newcomer	often	**P**	peg
millionaire	movie	news	oh	Pa	pen
mind	mow	newscast	oil	pack	pencil
mine	Mr.	newspaper	O.K.	package	penguin
miner	Mrs.	next	okay	pad	penny
minister	much	nibble	old	page	people
mink	mud	nice	on	paid	pep (py)
minnow	muffin	nickel	once	pail	pepper
mint	mule	nickname	one	pain (ful)	peppermint
minute	multiply	night	one-fourth	paint	perfume
miracle	multiplication	nightfall	oneself	pair	perhaps
mirror	mumps	nightmare	one-way	pajamas	period
misery	murder	nighttime	onion	pal	permit
mislay	museum	nine	only	palace	person
misplace	mush	nineteen	onward (s)	pale	personal
misprint	mushroom	ninety	open	pan	pest
miss (M)	music	ninth	operator	pancake	pet
missile	musical	nipple	opossum	panda	phone
misspell	musician	no	or	pants	phonograph
mist (y)	must (n't)	nobody	orange	papa	photo
mistake	mustard	nod	orbit	paper	photograph
mister	my	noise (y)	orchard	parade	piano
mitt	myself	none	order	pardon	pick
mitten	mystery	noodle	ordinary	parent	pickle
mix		noon	organ	park	picnic
mixture	**N**	normal	orphan	parrot	picture
mob	nail	north (ern)	ostrich	part	pie
model	name	nose	other	partner	piece
modern	nap	not	ouch	partnership	pig
moist	napkin	note	ought	party	pigeon
moisture	narrow	nothing	ounce	pass	pile
mom	nasty	notice	our	passenger	Pilgrim
moment	nation	November	ourselves	password	pill
Monday	nature	now	out (er)	past	pillow
money	naughty	nowhere	outdoors	paste	pilot
monkey	navy	number	outlaw	pasture	pimple
monster	near	nurse	outline	pat	pin
month	nearby	nursery	outside	patch	pine
moo	neat	nut	oven	path	pineapple
moon	neatness		over	pave	ping-pong
moonlight	necessary	**O**	overalls	paw	pingpong
moose	neck	oak	overboard	pay	pink
mop	necklace	oar	overcoat	payment	pint
more	necktie	oatmeal	overdo (done)	pea	pioneer
morning	need (n't)	oats	overeat	peace (ful)	pipe
most	needle	obey	overflow	peach	pistol
motel	Negro	ocean	overhead	peacock	pit
moth	neighbor	o'clock	overnight	peak	pitch
mother	neighborhood	October	overseas	peanut	pitcher
motion	neither	octopus	overtime	pear	pitiful
motor	nerve	odd	overweight	pearl	pity
motorcycle	nest	of	owe	pecan	pizza
mountain	net	of course	owl	peck	place
mouse	never	off	own	peek	plain
mouth	new	offer		peel	plan
movable	newborn	office		peep	plane

planet
plant
plantation
plaster
plate
play (ful)
playground
playhouse
playmate
plaything
pleasant
please
pleasure
plenty
plow
plug
plum
plumber
plus
P.M.
pocket
pocketbook
poem
point
poison
poke
pole
police (man)
polite
pond
pony
poodle
pool
poor
pop
popcorn
poppy
porch
pork
pose
possible
post
postage
postman
postmark
post office
postpone
pot
potato (es)
potato chip
pottery
pound
pour
powder
power (ful)
prairie

praise
pray (er)
prepare
present
President (p)
press
pretend
pretty
prevent
price
primary
prince
princess
print
prison
private
prize
problem
program
promise
promote
proof
property
protect
proud
prove
prune
public
puddle
puff
pull
pump
pumpkin
punch
punish
pup (py)
pupil
puppet
pure
purple
purse
push
puss (y)
put
puzzle

Q
quack (duck)
quarrel
quart
quarter
quarterback
queen
queer
question
quick (ly)

quiet
quilt
quit
quite

R
rabbit
raccoon
race
rack
radio
radish
rag
rail
railroad
rain (y)
rainbow
raindrop
raise
raisin
rake
ram
ran
ranch
rang
range
rap
rascal
rat
rate
rather
rattle
rattlesnake
raw
ray
rayon
razor
reach
read
ready
real
really
rear
reason
rebuild
receive
recess
record
red
redbird
redbreast
reflect
refresh (ment)
refrigerator
refuse
reindeer

rejoice
rejoin
related
religion
remain
remember
remind
remove
rent
repair
repay
repeat
report
respect
rest
restaurant
rest room
retire
return
review
reward
rhyme
rib
ribbon
rice
rich
rid
riddle
ride
right
rim
ring
rip
ripe
rise
river
road
roar
roast
rob
robber (y)
robe
robin
rock (y)
rocket
rode
roll
roller skate
romance
roof
room
rooster
root
rope
rose
rot

rotten
rough
round
route
row
rowboat
royal
rub
rubber
rug
rule
run
rung
rush
rust (y)

S
sack
sad (ness)
saddle
safe
safety
said
sail (or)
sailboat
saint
salad
sale
salt
same
sample
sand (y)
sandwich
sang
sank
sap
sat
satisfactory
Saturday
sauce
saucer
sausage
save
savings
saw
sawdust
say
scab
scale
scalp
scamper
scare (y)
scarecrow
scarf
scatter
school

schoolboy
schoolgirl
science
scissors
scoop
scooter
score
scout
scrap
scratch
scream
screen
screw
scrub
sea
seal
seam
search
seashore
season
seat
second
secret
see
seed
seem
seen
seesaw
selection
self, selves
selfish
sell
send (t)
sense
sensible
sentence
separate
September
servant
serve
service
set
settle
seven
seventeen
seventh
seventy
several
sew
shade (y)
shadow
shake
shall
shame
shampoo
shape

share	sixth	soil	spray	stool	sunset
sharp	sixty	sold	spread	stoop	sunshine
shave	size	soldier	spring	stop	supper
she ('d) ('ll)	skate	solid	sprinkle	stoplight	suppose
sheep	ski	solve	spy	store	sure
sheet	skin	some	square	storeroom	surface
shelf, shelves	skip	somebody	squash	stork	surfboard
shell	skirt	someone	squeak (y)	storm (y)	surgeon
shepherd	skunk	something	squeal	story	surprise
shine (y)	sky	sometime	squeeze	storyteller	surround
ship (ment)	skyscraper	somewhere	squirrel	stove	surroundings
shirt	slam	son	stab	straight (en)	suspect
shock	slap	song	stable	strange	swallow
shoe	slave	soon	stack	strap	swam
shoemaker	sled	sore	stage	straw	swamp
shook	sleep (y)	sorrow	stair	strawberry	swan
shoot	sleeve	sorry	stale	stream	swear
shop	sleigh	sort	stalk	street	sweat
shore	slept	soul	stamp	strength	sweater
short (ness)	slice	sound	stand	stretch	sweep
shot	slid	soup	star	strike	sweepstakes
should (n't)	slide	sour	starch	string	sweet (en)
shoulder	slim	south (ern)	stare	strip	sweetness
shout	slip	space	Stars & Stripes	stripe	sweetheart
shove	slipper	spaceship	start	strong	swell
shovel	slippery	spade	starve	stuck	swept
show (n)	slosh	spaghetti	state	student	swift
shower	slow (ly)	spank	station	studio	swim
shut	sly	spark	statue	study	swing
shutter	small	sparrow	stay	stuff	switch
shy	smart	speak	steak	stumble	sword
sick (ness)	smash	spear	steal	stung	syllable
side	smell	special	steam	stunt	
sidewalk	smile	speck	steel	style	T
sigh	smog	speech	steep	subject	table
sight	smoke (y)	speed	steeple	submarine	tablespoon
sign	smooth	speedometer	steer	subtract	tablet
silence	snack	spell	step	subtraction	tack
silent	snail	spend (t)	stepfather	such	taffy
silk	snake	spice	stepmother	suck	tag
sill	snap	spider	stereo	sudden (ly)	tail
silly	sneeze	spill	stew	suffer	tailor
silver	sniff	spin	stick	sugar	take (n)
simple	snow (y)	spirit	sticky	suit	tale
sin	snowball	spit	stiff	sum	talk
since	snowflake	splash	still	summer	tall
sing	snug	split	sting	sun (ny)	tame
single	so	spoil	stink	sunbeam	tan
sink	soak	spoke	stir	sunburn	tangle
sip	soap	sponge	stitch	Sunday	tank
sir	social	spook (y)	stock	sundown	tap
sis	sock	spool	stocking	sunflower	tape
sister	soda	spoon	stole (n)	sung	tar
sit	sofa	sport	stomach	sunk (en)	taste
six	soft	spot	stone	sunlight	tattle
sixteen	softball	sprain	stood	sunrise	tattletale

tattoo
taught
tax
taxpayer
tea
teach
teacher
team
teapot
tear
tease
teaspoon
teeth
telegram
telephone
telescope
television
tell
temper
temperature
ten
tend
tender
tennis
tent
tenth
term
terrible
test
than
thank (ful)
Thanksgiving
that ('s)
the
theater
their
them
then
there
there's
thermometer
these
they
they'd
they'll
they're
they've
thick
thief
thin
thing
think
third
thirst (y)
thirteen
thirty

this
thorn
those
thought (ful)
thoughtless
thousand
thread
three
threw
throat
throne
through
throw (n)
thumb
thunder
Thursday
tick
tick-tock
ticket
tickle
tiddlywinks
tie
tiger
tight
till
timber
time
tin
tinkle
tiny
tip
tiptoe
tire
tissue
title
to
toad
toast
tobacco
today
toe
together
toilet
told
tomato
tomorrow
ton
tone
tongue
tonight
too
took
tool
tooth
toothbrush
toothpaste

top
tore (n)
tornado
torpedo
tortoise
toss
total
touch
toward
towel
town
toy
trace
track
tractor
trade
traffic
trail
train
tramp
trap
trash
travel
tray
treasure
tree
trespass
trick
tricycle
trim
trip
trombone
troop
trophy
trouble
truck
true
truly
trumpet
trunk
trust
truth (ful)
try
tub
tube
Tuesday
tug
tulip
tumble
tune
tunnel
turkey
turn
turnip
turtle
TV

twelve
twenty
twice
twig
twin
twist
two
type
typewriter

U
ugly
umbrella
umpire
uncle
under
underline
understand
undershirt
underwear
undress
uneducated
unemployed
unfair
unfasten
unfinished
unfold
unfurnished
unhappy
uniform
United States
unkind
unknown
unnecessary
unsafe
untie
until
untrue
unwilling
unwise
unwrap
up
upon
upper
upset
upside down
upstairs
uptown
upward
us
U.S.
U.S.A.
use
useful
usher

V
vacant
vacation
Valentine
valley
valuable
value
vanish
varnish
vase
vegetable
velvet
verse
very
vessel
vest
vice-president
view
village
vine
violet
violin
visit (or)
vitamin
voice
volleyball
vote

W
waffle
wag
wagon
waist
wait
waiter
wake (n)
walk
wall
wallet
walnut
wander
want
war
warm
warmth
warn
wart
was (n't)
wash
washer
Washington, D.C.
George Washing-
ton
washroom
wasp
waste

watch
watchdog
water
waterfall
watermelon
waterproof
wave
wax
way
we ('ll) ('re)
weak (en) (ness)
wealth
weapon
wear
weather
weave
web
wedding
Wednesday
wee
weed
week
weekdays
weekend
weep
weigh (t)
welcome
well
went
were (n't)
west (ern)
wet
whale
what
wheat
wheel
wheelbarrow
when
where ('s)
which
while
whip
whirl
whirlpool
whirlwind
whisker
whisper
whistle
white
whiteness
who ('s)
whole
whom
whooping cough
whose
why

wicked	wine	won	worn	**X**	yonder
wide	wing	wonder (ful)	worry	Xmas	you ('d) ('ll)
wide-awake	wink	won't	worse (t)	X-ray	young
wife	winter	wood (en)	worth		youngster
wigwam	wipe	woodchuck	would (n't)	**Y**	your
wild	wire	woodpecker	wound	yard	yourself
wildcat	wise	woods	wrap	yarn	youth
wildlife	wish	woof	wreck	yawn	
will	witch	wool (en)	wren	year	**Z**
willing	with	word	wrist	yell	zebra
willow	without	wore	write (ten)	yellow (ish)	zero
win	woke	work	wrong	yes	zone
wind (y)	wolf, wolves	workman	wrote	yet	zoo
window	woman	world		yesterday	
windowpane	women	worm		yolk	

TABLE 1 FOR OBTAINING CLOZE SCORES

Number of complete sentences in sample

		1	2	3	4	5	6	7
	0	-5.00	29.50	41.00	46.75	50.20	52.50	54.14
	1	-5.95	28.55	40.05	45.80	49.25	51.55	53.19
	2	-6.90	27.60	39.10	44.85	48.30	50.60	52.24
	3	-7.85	26.65	38.15	43.90	47.35	49.65	51.29
	4	-8.80	25.70	37.20	42.95	46.40	48.70	50.34
	5	-9.75	24.75	36.25	42.00	45.45	47.75	49.39
	6	-10.70	23.80	35.30	41.05	44.50	46.80	48.44
	7	-11.65	22.85	34.35	40.10	43.55	45.85	47.49
	8	-12.60	21.90	33.40	39.15	42.60	44.90	46.54
	9	-13.55	20.95	32.45	38.20	41.65	43.95	45.59
	10	-14.50	20.00	31.50	37.25	40.70	43.00	44.64
	11	-15.45	19.05	30.55	36.30	39.75	42.05	43.69
	12	-16.40	18.10	29.60	35.35	38.80	41.10	42.74
	13	-17.35	17.15	28.65	34.40	37.85	40.15	41.79
	14	-18.30	16.20	27.70	33.45	36.90	39.20	40.84
Number of unfamiliar words in sample	15	-19.25	15.25	26.75	32.50	35.95	38.25	39.89
	16	-20.20	14.30	25.80	31.55	35.00	37.30	38.94
	17	-21.15	13.35	24.85	30.60	34.05	36.35	37.99
	18	-22.10	12.40	23.90	29.65	33.10	35.40	37.04
	19	-23.05	11.45	22.95	28.70	32.15	34.45	36.09
	20	-24.00	10.50	22.00	27.75	31.20	33.50	35.14
	21	-24.95	9.55	21.05	26.80	30.25	32.55	34.19
	22	-25.90	8.60	20.10	25.85	29.30	31.60	33.24
	23	-26.85	7.65	19.15	24.90	28.35	30.65	32.29
	24	-27.80	6.70	18.20	23.95	27.40	29.70	31.34
	25	-28.75	5.75	17.25	23.00	26.45	28.75	30.39
	26	-29.70	4.80	16.30	22.05	25.50	27.80	29.44
	27	-30.65	3.85	15.35	21.10	24.55	26.85	28.49
	28	-31.60	2.90	14.40	20.15	23.60	25.90	27.54
	29	-32.55	1.95	13.45	19.20	22.65	24.95	26.59
	30	-33.50	1.00	12.50	18.25	21.70	24.00	25.64
	31	-34.45	0.05	11.55	17.30	20.75	23.05	24.69
	32	-35.40	-0.90	10.60	16.35	19.80	22.10	23.74
	33	-36.35	-1.85	9.65	15.40	18.85	21.15	22.79
	34	-37.30	-2.80	8.70	14.45	17.90	20.20	21.84
	35	-38.25	-3.75	7.75	13.50	16.95	19.25	20.89
	36	-39.20	-4.70	6.80	12.55	16.00	18.30	19.94
	37	-40.15	-5.65	5.85	11.60	15.05	17.35	18.99
	38	-41.10	-6.60	4.90	10.65	14.10	16.40	18.04
	39	-42.05	-7.55	3.95	9.70	13.15	15.45	17.09
	40	-43.00	-8.50	3.00	8.75	12.20	14.50	16.14
	41	-43.95	-9.45	2.05	7.80	11.25	13.55	15.19
	42	-44.90	-10.40	1.10	6.85	10.30	12.60	14.24
	43	-45.85	-11.35	0.15	5.90	9.35	11.65	13.29
	44	-46.80	-12.30	-0.80	4.95	8.40	10.70	12.34
	45	-47.75	-13.25	-1.75	4.00	7.45	9.75	11.39
	46	-48.70	-14.20	-2.70	3.05	6.50	8.80	10.44
	47	-49.65	-15.15	-3.65	2.10	5.55	7.85	9.49
	48	-50.60	-16.10	-4.60	1.15	4.60	6.90	8.54
	49	-51.55	-17.05	-5.55	0.20	3.65	5.95	7.59
	50	-52.50	-18.00	-6.50	-0.75	2.70	5.00	6.64

TABLE 1 CONTINUED

Number of complete sentences in sample

	8	9	10	11	12	13	14
0	55.38	56.33	57.10	57.73	58.25	58.69	59.07
1	54.42	55.38	56.15	56.78	57.30	57.74	58.12
2	53.47	54.43	55.20	55.83	56.35	56.79	57.17
3	52.52	53.48	54.25	54.88	55.40	55.84	56.22
4	51.57	52.53	53.30	53.93	54.45	54.89	55.27
5	50.63	51.58	52.35	52.98	53.50	53.94	54.32
6	49.67	50.63	51.40	52.03	52.55	52.99	53.37
7	48.72	49.68	50.45	51.08	51.60	52.04	52.42
8	47.77	48.73	49.50	50.13	50.65	51.09	51.47
9	46.82	47.78	48.55	49.18	49.70	50.14	50.52
10	45.88	46.83	47.60	48.23	48.75	49.19	49.57
11	44.92	45.88	46.65	47.28	47.80	48.24	48.62
12	43.97	44.93	45.70	46.33	46.85	47.29	47.67
13	43.02	43.98	44.75	45.38	45.90	46.34	46.72
14	42.07	43.03	43.80	44.43	44.95	45.39	45.77
15	41.13	42.08	42.85	43.48	44.00	44.44	44.82
16	40.17	41.13	41.90	42.53	43.05	43.49	43.87
17	39.23	40.18	40.95	41.58	42.10	42.54	42.92
18	38.28	39.23	40.00	40.63	41.15	41.59	41.97
19	37.33	38.28	39.05	39.68	40.20	40.64	41.02
20	36.38	37.33	38.10	38.73	39.25	39.69	40.07
21	35.43	36.38	37.15	37.78	38.30	38.74	39.12
22	34.48	35.43	36.20	36.83	37.35	37.79	38.17
23	33.53	34.48	35.25	35.88	36.40	36.84	37.22
24	32.58	33.53	34.30	34.93	35.45	35.89	36.27
25	31.63	32.58	33.35	33.98	34.50	34.94	35.32
26	30.68	31.63	32.40	33.03	33.55	33.99	34.37
27	29.73	30.68	31.45	32.08	32.60	33.04	33.42
28	28.78	29.73	30.50	31.13	31.65	32.09	32.47
29	27.83	28.78	29.55	30.18	30.70	31.14	31.52
30	26.88	27.83	28.60	29.23	29.75	30.19	30.57
31	25.93	26.88	27.65	28.28	28.80	29.24	29.62
32	24.98	25.93	26.70	27.33	27.85	28.29	28.67
33	24.03	24.98	25.75	26.38	26.90	27.34	27.72
34	23.08	24.03	24.80	25.43	25.95	26.39	26.77
35	22.13	23.08	23.85	24.48	25.00	25.44	25.82
36	21.18	22.13	22.90	23.53	24.05	24.49	24.87
37	20.23	21.18	21.95	22.58	23.10	23.54	23.92
38	19.28	20.23	21.00	21.63	22.15	22.59	22.97
39	18.33	19.28	20.05	20.68	21.20	21.64	22.02
40	17.38	18.33	19.10	19.73	20.25	20.69	21.07
41	16.43	17.38	18.15	18.78	19.30	19.74	20.12
42	15.48	16.43	17.20	17.83	18.35	18.79	19.17
43	14.53	15.48	16.25	16.88	17.40	17.84	18.22
44	13.58	14.53	15.30	15.93	16.45	16.89	17.27
45	12.63	13.58	14.35	14.98	15.50	15.94	16.32
46	11.68	12.63	13.40	14.03	14.55	14.99	15.37
47	10.73	11.68	12.45	13.08	13.60	14.04	14.42
48	9.78	10.73	11.50	12.13	12.65	13.09	13.47
49	8.83	9.78	10.55	11.18	11.70	12.14	12.52
50	7.88	8.83	9.60	10.23	10.75	11.19	11.57

Number of unfamiliar words sample

TABLE 1 CONTINUED

Number of complete sentences in sample

	15	16	17	18	19	20	21
0	59.40	59.69	59.94	60.17	60.37	60.55	60.71
1	58.45	58.74	58.99	59.22	59.42	59.60	59.76
2	57.50	57.79	58.04	58.27	58.47	58.65	58.81
3	56.55	56.84	57.09	57.32	57.52	57.70	57.86
4	55.60	55.89	56.14	56.37	56.57	56.75	56.91
5	54.65	54.94	55.19	55.42	55.62	55.80	55.96
6	53.70	53.99	54.24	54.47	54.67	54.85	55.01
7	52.75	53.04	53.29	53.52	53.72	53.90	54.06
8	51.80	52.09	52.34	52.57	52.77	52.95	53.11
9	50.85	51.14	51.39	51.62	51.82	52.00	52.16
10	49.90	50.19	50.44	50.67	50.87	51.05	51.21
11	48.95	49.24	49.49	49.72	49.92	50.10	50.26
12	48.00	48.29	48.54	48.77	48.97	49.15	49.31
13	47.05	47.34	47.59	47.82	48.02	48.20	48.36
14	46.10	46.39	46.64	46.87	47.07	47.25	47.41
15	45.15	45.44	45.69	45.92	46.12	46.30	46.46
16	44.20	44.49	44.74	44.97	45.17	45.35	45.51
17	43.25	43.54	43.79	44.02	44.22	44.40	44.56
18	42.30	42.59	42.84	43.07	43.27	43.45	43.61
19	41.35	41.64	41.89	42.12	42.32	42.50	42.66
20	40.40	40.69	40.94	41.17	41.37	41.55	41.71
21	39.45	39.74	39.99	40.22	40.42	40.60	40.76
22	38.50	38.79	39.04	39.27	39.47	39.65	39.81
23	37.55	37.84	38.09	38.32	38.52	38.70	38.86
24	36.60	36.89	37.14	37.37	37.57	37.75	37.91
25	35.65	35.94	36.19	36.42	36.62	36.80	36.96
26	34.70	34.99	35.24	35.47	35.67	35.85	36.01
27	33.75	34.04	34.29	34.52	34.72	34.90	35.06
28	32.80	33.09	33.34	33.57	33.77	33.95	34.11
29	31.85	32.14	32.39	32.62	32.82	33.00	33.16
30	30.90	31.19	31.44	31.67	31.87	32.05	32.21
31	29.95	30.24	30.49	30.72	30.92	31.10	31.26
32	29.00	29.29	29.54	29.77	29.97	30.15	30.31
33	28.05	28.34	28.59	28.82	29.02	29.20	29.36
34	27.10	27.39	27.64	27.87	28.07	28.25	28.41
35	26.15	26.44	26.69	26.92	27.12	27.30	27.46
36	25.20	25.49	25.74	25.97	26.17	26.35	26.51
37	24.25	24.54	24.79	25.02	25.22	25.40	25.56
38	23.30	23.59	23.84	24.07	24.27	24.45	24.61
39	22.35	22.64	22.89	23.12	23.32	23.50	23.66
40	21.40	21.69	21.94	22.17	22.37	22.55	22.71
41	20.45	20.74	20.99	21.22	21.42	21.60	21.76
42	19.50	19.79	20.04	20.27	20.47	20.65	20.81
43	18.55	18.84	19.09	19.32	19.52	19.70	19.86
44	17.60	17.89	18.14	18.37	18.57	18.75	18.91
45	16.65	16.94	17.19	17.42	17.62	17.80	17.96
46	15.70	15.99	16.24	16.47	16.67	16.85	17.01
47	14.75	15.04	15.29	15.52	15.72	15.90	16.06
48	13.80	14.09	14.34	14.57	14.77	14.95	15.11
49	12.85	13.14	13.39	13.62	13.82	14.00	14.16
50	11.90	12.19	12.44	12.67	12.87	13.05	13.21

Number of unfamiliar words in sample

TABLE 1 CONTINUED

Number of complete sentences in sample

	22	23	24	25	26	27	28
0	60.86	61.00	61.13	61.24	61.35	61.44	61.54
1	59.91	60.05	60.17	60.29	60.40	60.49	60.59
2	58.96	59.10	59.22	59.34	59.45	59.54	59.64
3	58.01	58.15	58.27	58.39	58.50	58.59	58.69
4	57.06	57.20	57.32	57.44	57.55	57.64	57.74
5	56.11	56.25	56.38	56.49	56.60	56.69	56.79
6	55.16	55.30	55.42	55.54	55.65	55.74	55.84
7	54.21	54.35	54.47	54.59	54.70	54.79	54.89
8	53.26	53.40	53.52	53.64	53.75	53.84	53.94
9	52.31	52.45	52.57	52.69	52.80	52.89	52.99
10	51.36	51.50	51.63	51.74	51.85	51.94	52.04
11	50.41	50.55	50.67	50.79	50.90	50.99	51.09
12	49.46	49.60	49.72	49.84	49.95	50.04	50.14
13	48.51	48.65	48.77	48.89	49.00	49.09	49.19
14	47.56	47.70	47.82	47.94	48.05	48.14	48.24
15	46.61	46.75	46.88	46.99	47.10	47.19	47.29
16	45.66	45.80	45.92	46.04	46.15	46.24	46.34
17	44.71	44.85	44.98	45.09	45.20	45.29	45.39
18	43.76	43.90	44.03	44.14	44.25	44.34	44.44
19	42.81	42.95	43.08	43.19	43.30	43.39	43.49
20	41.86	42.00	42.13	42.24	42.35	42.44	42.54
21	40.91	41.05	41.18	41.29	41.40	41.49	41.59
22	39.96	40.10	40.23	40.34	40.45	40.54	40.64
23	39.01	39.15	39.28	39.39	39.50	39.59	39.69
24	38.06	38.20	38.33	38.44	38.55	38.64	38.74
25	37.11	37.25	37.38	37.49	37.60	37.69	37.79
26	36.16	36.30	36.43	36.54	36.65	36.74	36.84
27	35.21	35.35	35.48	35.59	35.70	35.79	35.89
28	34.26	34.40	34.53	34.64	34.75	34.84	34.94
29	33.31	33.45	33.58	33.69	33.80	33.89	33.99
30	32.36	32.50	32.63	32.74	32.85	32.94	33.04
31	31.41	31.55	31.68	31.79	31.90	31.99	32.09
32	30.46	30.60	30.73	30.84	30.95	31.04	31.14
33	29.51	29.65	29.78	29.89	30.00	30.09	30.19
34	28.56	28.70	28.83	28.94	29.05	29.14	29.24
35	27.61	27.75	27.88	27.99	28.10	28.19	28.29
36	26.66	26.80	26.93	27.04	27.15	27.24	27.34
37	25.71	25.85	25.98	26.09	26.20	26.29	26.39
38	24.76	24.90	25.03	25.14	25.25	25.34	25.44
39	23.81	23.95	24.08	24.19	24.30	24.39	24.49
40	22.86	23.00	23.13	23.24	23.35	23.44	23.54
41	21.91	22.05	22.18	22.29	22.40	22.49	22.59
42	20.96	21.10	21.23	21.34	21.45	21.54	21.64
43	20.01	20.15	20.28	20.39	20.50	20.59	20.69
44	19.06	19.20	19.33	19.44	19.55	19.64	19.74
45	18.11	18.25	18.38	18.49	18.60	18.69	18.79
46	17.16	17.30	17.43	17.54	17.65	17.74	17.84
47	16.21	16.35	16.48	16.59	16.70	16.79	16.89
48	15.26	15.40	15.53	15.64	15.75	15.84	15.94
49	14.31	14.45	14.58	14.69	14.80	14.89	14.99
50	13.36	13.50	13.63	13.74	13.85	13.94	14.04

Number of unfamiliar words in sample

TABLE 1 CONTINUED

Number of complete sentences in sample

	29	30	31	32	33	34	35
0	61.62	61.70	61.77	61.84	61.91	61.97	62.03
1	60.67	60.75	60.82	60.89	60.96	61.02	61.08
2	59.72	59.80	59.87	59.94	60.01	60.07	60.13
3	58.77	58.85	58.92	58.99	59.06	59.12	59.18
4	57.82	57.90	57.97	58.04	58.11	58.17	58.23
5	56.87	56.95	57.02	57.09	57.16	57.22	57.28
6	55.92	56.00	56.07	56.14	56.21	56.27	56.33
7	54.97	55.05	55.12	55.19	55.26	55.32	55.38
8	54.02	54.10	54.17	54.24	54.31	54.37	54.43
9	53.07	53.15	53.22	53.29	53.36	53.42	53.48
10	52.12	52.20	52.27	52.34	52.41	52.47	52.53
11	51.17	51.25	51.32	51.39	51.46	51.52	51. 58
12	50.22	50.30	50.37	50.44	50.51	50.57	50.63
13	49.27	49.35	49.42	49.49	49.56	49.62	49.68
14	48.32	48.40	48.47	48.54	48.61	48.67	48.73
15	47.37	47.45	47.52	47.59	47.66	47.72	47.78
16	46.42	46.50	46.57	46.64	46.71	46.77	46.83
17	45.47	45.55	45.62	45.69	45.76	45.82	45.88
18	44.52	44.60	44.67	44.74	44.81	44.87	44.93
19	43.57	43.65	43.72	43.79	43.86	43.92	43.98
20	42.62	42.70	42.77	42.84	42.91	42.97	43.03
21	41.67	41.75	41.82	41.89	41.96	42.02	42.08
22	40.72	40.80	40.87	40.94	41.01	41.07	41.13
23	39.77	39.85	39.92	39.99	40.06	40.12	40.18
24	38.82	38.90	38.97	39.04	39.11	39.17	39.23
25	37.87	37.95	38.02	38.09	38.16	38.22	38.28
26	36.92	37.00	37.07	37.14	37.21	37.27	37.33
27	35.97	36.05	36.12	36.19	36.26	36.32	36.38
28	35.02	35.10	35.17	35.24	35.31	35.37	35.43
29	34.07	34.15	34.22	34.29	34.36	34.42	34.48
30	33.12	33.20	33.27	33.34	33.41	33.47	33.53
31	32.17	32.25	32.32	32.39	32.46	32.52	32.58
32	31.22	31.30	31.37	31.44	31.51	31.57	31.63
33	30.27	30.35	30.42	30.49	30.56	30.62	30.68
34	29.32	29.40	29.47	29.54	29.61	29.67	29.73
35	28.37	28.45	28.52	28.59	28.66	28.72	28.78
36	27.42	27.50	27.57	27.64	27.71	27.77	27.83
37	26.47	26.55	26.62	26.69	26.76	26.82	26.88
38	25.52	25.60	25.67	25.74	25.81	25.87	25.93
39	24.57	24.65	24.72	24.79	24.86	24.92	24.98
40	23.62	23.70	23.77	23.84	23.91	23.97	24.03
41	22.67	22.75	22.82	22.89	22.96	23.02	23.08
42	21.72	21.80	21.87	21.94	22.01	22.07	22.13
43	20.77	20.85	20.92	20.99	21.06	21.12	21.18
44	19.82	19.90	19.97	20.04	20.11	20.17	20.23
45	18.87	18.95	19.02	19.09	19.16	19.22	19.28
46	17.92	18.00	18.07	18.14	18.21	18.27	18.33
47	16.97	17.05	17.12	17.19	17.26	17.32	17.38
48	16.02	16.10	16.17	16.24	16.31	16.37	16.43
49	15.07	15.15	15.22	15.29	15.36	15.42	15.48
50	14.12	14.20	14.27	14.34	14.41	14.47	14.53

Number of unfamiliar words in sample

TABLE 1 CONTINUED

Number of complete sentences in sample

Number of unfamiliar words in sample	36	37	38	39	40
0	62.08	62.14	62.18	62.23	62.27
1	61.13	61.19	61.23	61.28	61.32
2	60.18	60.24	60.28	60.33	60.37
3	59.23	59.29	59.33	59.38	59.42
4	58.28	58.34	58.38	58.43	58.47
5	57.33	57.39	57.43	57.48	57.52
6	56.38	56.44	56.48	56.53	56.57
7	55.43	55.49	55.53	55.58	55.62
8	54.48	54.54	54.58	54.63	54.67
9	53.53	53.59	53.63	53.68	53.72
10	52.58	52.64	52.68	52.73	52.77
11	51.63	51.69	51.73	51.78	51.82
12	50.68	50.74	50.78	50.83	50.87
13	49.73	49.79	49.83	49.88	49.92
14	48.78	48.84	48.88	48.93	48.97
15	47.83	47.89	47.93	47.98	48.02
16	46.88	46.94	46.98	47.03	47.07
17	45.93	45.99	46.03	46.08	46.13
18	44.98	45.04	45.08	45.13	45.18
19	44.03	44.09	44.13	44.18	44.23
20	43.08	43.14	43.18	43.23	43.28
21	42.13	42.19	42.23	42.28	42.32
22	41.18	41.24	41.28	41.33	41.38
23	40.23	40.29	40.33	40.38	40.43
24	39.28	39.34	39.38	39.43	39.48
25	38.33	38.39	38.43	38.48	38.53
26	37.38	37.44	37.48	37.53	37.57
27	36.43	36.49	36.53	36.58	36.63
28	35.48	35.54	35.58	35.63	35.68
29	34.53	34.59	34.63	34.68	34.73
30	33.58	33.64	33.68	33.73	33.78
31	32.63	32.69	32.73	32.78	32.82
32	31.68	31.74	31.78	31.83	31.88
33	30.73	30.79	30.83	30.88	30.93
34	29.78	29.84	29.88	29.93	29.98
35	28.83	28.89	28.93	28.98	29.03
36	27.88	27.94	27.98	28.03	28.07
37	26.93	26.99	27.03	27.08	27.13
38	25.98	26.04	26.08	26.13	26.18
39	25.03	25.09	25.13	25.18	25.23
40	24.08	24.14	24.18	24.23	24.28
41	23.13	23.19	23.23	23.28	23.32
42	22.18	22.24	22.28	22.33	22.38
43	21.23	21.29	21.33	21.38	21.43
44	20.28	20.34	20.38	20.43	20.48
45	19.33	19.39	19.43	19.48	19.53
46	18.38	18.44	18.48	18.53	18.57
47	17.43	17.49	17.53	17.58	17.63
48	16.48	16.54	16.58	16.63	16.68
49	15.53	15.59	15.63	15.68	15.73
50	14.58	14.64	14.68	14.73	14.78

TABLE 1 CONTINUED

Number of complete sentences in sample

	41	42	43	44	45
0	62.32	62.36	62.40	62.43	62.47
1	61.37	61.41	61.45	61.48	61.52
2	60.42	60.46	60.50	60.53	60.57
3	59.47	59.51	59.55	59.58	59.62
4	58.52	58.56	58.60	58.63	58.67
5	57.57	57.61	57.65	57.68	57.72
6	56.62	56.66	56.70	56.73	56.77
7	55.67	55.71	55.75	55.78	55.82
8	54.72	54.76	54.80	54.83	54.87
9	53.77	53.81	53.85	53.88	53.92
10	52.82	52.86	52.90	52.93	52.97
11	51.87	51.91	51.95	51.98	52.02
12	50.92	50.96	51.00	51.03	51.07
13	49.97	50.01	50.05	50.08	50.12
14	49.02	49.06	49.10	49.13	49.17
15	48.07	48.11	48.15	48.18	48.22
16	47.12	47.16	47.20	47.23	47.27
17	46.17	46.21	46.25	46.28	46.32
18	45.22	45.26	45.30	45.33	45.37
19	44.27	44.31	44.35	44.38	44.42
20	43.32	43.36	43.40	43.43	43.47
21	42.37	42.41	42.45	42.48	42.52
22	41.42	41.46	41.50	41.53	41.57
23	40.47	40.51	40.55	40.58	40.62
24	39.52	39.56	39.60	39.63	39.67
25	38.57	38.61	38.65	38.68	38.72
26	37.62	37.66	37.70	37.73	37.77
27	36.67	36.71	36.75	36.78	36.82
28	35.72	35.76	35.80	35.83	35.87
29	34.77	34.81	34.85	34.88	34.92
30	33.82	33.86	33.90	33.93	33.97
31	32.87	32.91	32.95	32.98	33.02
32	31.92	31.96	32.00	32.03	32.07
33	30.97	31.01	31.05	31.08	31.12
34	30.02	30.16	30.10	30.13	30.17
35	29.07	29.11	29.15	29.18	29.22
36	28.12	28.16	28.20	28.23	28.27
37	27.17	27.21	27.25	27.28	27.32
38	26.22	26.26	26.30	26.33	26.37
39	25.27	25.31	25.35	25.38	25.42
40	24.32	24.36	24.40	24.43	24.47
41	23.37	23.41	23.45	23.48	23.52
42	22.42	22.46	22.50	22.53	22.57
43	21.47	21.51	21.55	21.58	21.62
44	20.52	20.56	20.60	20.63	20.67
45	19.57	19.61	19.65	19.68	19.72
46	18.62	18.66	18.70	18.73	18.77
47	17.67	17.71	17.75	17.78	17.82
48	16.72	16.76	16.80	16.83	16.87
49	15.77	15.81	15.85	15.88	15.92
50	14.82	14.86	14.90	14.93	14.97

Number of unfamiliar words in sample

TABLE 1 CONTINUED

Number of complete sentences in sample

	46	47	48	49	50
0	62.50	62.53	62.56	62.59	62.62
1	61.55	61.58	61.61	61.64	61.67
2	60.60	60.63	60.66	60.69	60.72
3	59.65	59.68	59.71	59.74	59.77
4	58.70	58.73	58.76	58.79	58.82
5	57.75	57.78	57.81	57.84	57.87
6	56.80	56.83	56.86	56.89	56.92
7	55.85	55.88	55.91	55.94	55.97
8	54.90	54.93	54.96	54.99	55.02
9	53.95	53.98	54.01	54.04	54.07
10	53.00	53.03	53.06	53.09	53.12
11	52.05	52.08	52.11	52.14	52.17
12	51.10	51.13	51.16	51.19	51.22
13	50.15	50.18	50.21	50.24	50.27
14	49.20	49.23	49.26	49.29	49.32
15	48.25	48.28	48.31	48.34	48.37
16	47.30	47.33	47.36	47.39	47.42
17	46.35	46.38	46.41	46.44	46.47
18	45.40	45.43	45.46	45.49	45.52
19	44.45	44.48	44.51	44.54	44.57
20	43.50	43.53	43.56	43.59	43.62
21	42.55	42.58	42.61	42.64	42.67
22	41.60	41.63	41.66	41.69	41.72
23	40.65	40.68	40.71	40.74	40.77
24	39.70	39.73	39.76	39.79	39.82
25	38.75	38.78	38.81	38.84	38.87
26	37.80	37.83	37.86	37.89	37.92
27	36.85	36.88	36.91	36.94	36.97
28	35.90	35.93	35.96	35.99	36.02
29	34.95	34.98	35.01	35.04	35.07
30	34.00	34.03	34.06	34.09	34.12
31	33.05	33.08	33.11	33.14	33.17
32	32.10	32.13	32.16	32.19	32.22
33	31.15	31.18	31.21	31.24	31.27
34	30.20	30.23	30.26	30.29	30.32
35	29.25	29.28	29.31	29.34	29.37
36	28.30	28.33	28.36	28.39	28.42
37	27.35	27.38	27.41	27.44	27.47
38	26.40	26.43	26.46	26.49	26.52
39	25.45	25.48	25.51	25.54	25.57
40	24.50	24.53	24.56	24.59	24.62
41	23.55	23.58	23.61	23.64	23.67
42	22.60	22.63	22.66	22.69	22.72
43	21.65	21.68	21.71	21.74	21.77
44	20.70	20.73	20.76	20.79	20.82
45	19.75	19.78	19.81	19.84	19.87
46	18.80	18.83	18.86	18.89	18.92
47	17.85	17.88	17.91	17.94	17.97
48	16.90	16.93	16.96	16.99	17.02
49	15.95	15.98	16.01	16.04	16.07
50	15.00	15.03	15.06	15.09	15.12

Number of unfamiliar words in sample

TABLE 2 FOR OBTAINING READING LEVELS

Number of sentences in sample

Number of unfamiliar words in sample	1	2	3	4	5	6	7	8
0	16	9-10	5-6	4	3	3	2	2
1	16	9-10	5-6	4	3	3	2	2
2	16	9-10	5-6	4	4	3	3	2
3	16	11-12	7-8	5-6	4	3	3	3
4	16	11-12	7-8	5-6	4	4	3	3
5	16	11-12	7-8	5-6	4	4	3	3
6	16	11-12	7-8	5-6	4	4	4	3
7	16	11-12	7-8	5-6	5-6	4	4	4
8	16	11-12	7-8	5-6	5-6	4	4	4
9	16	13-15	9-10	7-8	5-6	5-6	4	4
10	16	13-15	9-10	7-8	5-6	5-6	4	4
11	16	13-15	9-10	7-8	5-6	5-6	5-6	4
12	16	13-15	9-10	7-8	7-8	5-6	5-6	5-6
13	16	13-15	9-10	7-8	7-8	5-6	5-6	5-6
14	16	13-15	9-10	7-8	7-8	5-6	5-6	5-6
15	16	13-15	11-12	9-10	7-8	7-8	5-6	5-6
16	16	16	11-12	9-10	7-8	7-8	7-8	5-6
17	16	16	11-12	9-10	7-8	7-8	7-8	5-6
18	16	16	11-12	9-10	7-8	7-8	7-8	7-8
19	16	16	11-12	9-10	9-10	7-8	7-8	7-8
20	16	16	11-12	9-10	9-10	7-8	7-8	7-8
21	16	16	11-12	11-12	9-10	9-10	7-8	7-8
22	16	16	13-15	11-12	9-10	9-10	7-8	7-8
23	16	16	13-15	11-12	9-10	9-10	9-10	7-8
24	16	16	13-15	11-12	9-10	9-10	9-10	9-10
25	16	16	13-15	11-12	11-12	9-10	9-10	9-10
26	16	16	13-15	11-12	11-12	9-10	9-10	9-10
27	16	16	13-15	11-12	11-12	11-12	9-10	9-10
28	16	16	16	13-15	11-12	11-12	9-10	9-10
29	16	16	16	13-15	11-12	11-12	11-12	9-10
30	16	16	16	13-15	11-12	11-12	11-12	11-12
31	16	16	16	13-15	13-15	11-12	11-12	11-12
32	16	16	16	13-15	13-15	11-12	11-12	11-12
33	16	16	16	13-15	13-15	11-12	11-12	11-12
34	16	16	16	16	13-15	13-15	11-12	11-12
35	16	16	16	16	13-15	13-15	13-15	11-12
36	16	16	16	16	13-15	13-15	13-15	11-12
37	16	16	16	16	13-15	13-15	13-15	13-15
38	16	16	16	16	16	13-15	13-15	13-15
39	16	16	16	16	16	13-15	13-15	13-15
40	16	16	16	16	16	16	13-15	13-15
41	16	16	16	16	16	16	13-15	13-15
42	16	16	16	16	16	16	16	13-15
43	16	16	16	16	16	16	16	16
44	16	16	16	16	16	16	16	16
45	16	16	16	16	16	16	16	16
46	16	16	16	16	16	16	16	16
47	16	16	16	16	16	16	16	16
48	16	16	16	16	16	16	16	16
49	16	16	16	16	16	16	16	16
50	16	16	16	16	16	16	16	16

TABLE 2 CONTINUED

Number of sentences in sample

Number of unfamiliar words in sample	9	10	11	12	13	14	15	16
0	1	1	1	1	1	1	1	1
1	2	1	1	1	1	1	1	1
2	2	2	2	2	1	1	1	1
3	2	2	2	2	2	1	1	1
4	3	2	2	2	2	2	2	2
5	3	3	3	2	2	2	2	2
6	3	3	3	3	3	2	2	2
7	3	3	3	3	3	3	3	2
8	4	3	3	3	3	3	3	3
9	4	4	3	3	3	3	3	3
10	4	4	4	4	3	3	3	3
11	4	4	4	4	4	4	4	3
12	4	4	4	4	4	4	4	4
13	5-6	4	4	4	4	4	4	4
14	5-6	5-6	4	4	4	4	4	4
15	5-6	5-6	5-6	5-6	4	4	4	4
16	5-6	5-6	5-6	5-6	5-6	5-6	4	4
17	5-6	5-6	5-6	5-6	5-6	5-6	5-6	5-6
18	5-6	5-6	5-6	5-6	5-6	5-6	5-6	5-6
19	7-8	5-6	5-6	5-6	5-6	5-6	5-6	5-6
20	7-8	7-8	7-8	5-6	5-6	5-6	5-6	5-6
21	7-8	7-8	7-8	7-8	7-8	5-6	5-6	5-6
22	7-8	7-8	7-8	7-8	7-8	7-8	7-8	7-8
23	7-8	7-8	7-8	7-8	7-8	7-8	7-8	7-8
24	7-8	7-8	7-8	7-8	7-8	7-8	7-8	7-8
25	9-10	7-8	7-8	7-8	7-8	7-8	7-8	7-8
26	9-10	9-10	7-8	7-8	7-8	7-8	7-8	7-8
27	9-10	9-10	9-10	9-10	7-8	7-8	7-8	7-8
28	9-10	9-10	9-10	9-10	9-10	9-10	9-10	7-8
29	9-10	9-10	9-10	9-10	9-10	9-10	9-10	9-10
30	9-10	9-10	9-10	9-10	9-10	9-10	9-10	9-10
31	11-12	9-10	9-10	9-10	9-10	9-10	9-10	9-10
32	11-12	11-12	9-10	9-10	9-10	9-10	9-10	9-10
33	11-12	11-12	11-12	11-12	9-10	9-10	9-10	9-10
34	11-12	11-12	11-12	11-12	11-12	11-12	9-10	9-10
35	11-12	11-12	11-12	11-12	11-12	11-12	11-12	11-12
36	11-12	11-12	11-12	11-12	11-12	11-12	11-12	11-12
37	11-12	11-12	11-12	11-12	11-12	11-12	11-12	11-12
38	13-15	13-15	11-12	11-12	11-12	11-12	11-12	11-12
39	13-15	13-15	13-15	11-12	11-12	11-12	11-12	11-12
40	13-15	13-15	13-15	13-15	13-15	11-12	11-12	11-12
41	13-15	13-15	13-15	13-15	13-15	13-15	13-15	13-15
42	13-15	13-15	13-15	13-15	13-15	13-15	13-15	13-15
43	13-15	13-15	13-15	13-15	13-15	13-15	13-15	13-15
44	16	13-15	13-15	13-15	13-15	13-15	13-15	13-15
45	16	16	16	13-15	13-15	13-15	13-15	13-15
46	16	16	16	16	16	13-15	13-15	13-15
47	16	16	16	16	16	16	16	13-15
48	16	16	16	16	16	16	16	16
49	16	16	16	16	16	16	16	16
50	16	16	16	16	16	16	16	16

TABLE 2 CONTINUED

Number of sentences in sample

Number of unfamiliar words in sample	17	18	19	20	21	22	23	24
0	1	1	1	1	1	1	1	1
1	1	1	1	1	1	1	1	1
2	1	1	1	1	1	1	1	1
3	1	1	1	1	1	1	1	1
4	1	1	1	1	1	1	1	1
5	2	2	2	2	2	1	1	1
6	2	2	2	2	2	2	2	2
7	2	2	2	2	2	2	2	2
8	3	3	3	3	2	2	2	2
9	3	3	3	3	3	3	3	3
10	3	3	3	3	3	3	3	3
11	3	3	3	3	3	3	3	3
12	4	4	4	3	3	3	3	3
13	4	4	4	4	4	4	4	4
14	4	4	4	4	4	4	4	4
15	4	4	4	4	4	4	4	4
16	4	4	4	4	4	4	4	4
17	5-6	4	4	4	4	4	4	4
18	5-6	5-6	5-6	5-6	5-6	5-6	5-6	4
19	5-6	5-6	5-6	5-6	5-6	5-6	5-6	5-6
20	5-6	5-6	5-6	5-6	5-6	5-6	5-6	5-6
21	5-6	5-6	5-6	5-6	5-6	5-6	5-6	5-6
22	5-6	5-6	5-6	5-6	5-6	5-6	5-6	5-6
23	7-8	7-8	7-8	7-8	7-8	5-6	5-6	5-6
24	7-8	7-8	7-8	7-8	7-8	7-8	7-8	7-8
25	7-8	7-8	7-8	7-8	7-8	7-8	7-8	7-8
26	7-8	7-8	7-8	7-8	7-8	7-8	7-8	7-8
27	7-8	7-8	7-8	7-8	7-8	7-8	7-8	7-8
28	7-8	7-8	7-8	7-8	7-8	7-8	7-8	7-8
29	9-10	9-10	9-10	9-10	7-8	7-8	7-8	7-8
30	9-10	9-10	9-10	9-10	9-10	9-10	9-10	9-10
31	9-10	9-10	9-10	9-10	9-10	9-10	9-10	9-10
32	9-10	9-10	9-10	9-10	9-10	9-10	9-10	9-10
33	9-10	9-10	9-10	9-10	9-10	9-10	9-10	9-10
34	9-10	9-10	9-10	9-10	9-10	9-10	9-10	9-10
35	11-12	11-12	9-10	9-10	9-10	9-10	9-10	9-10
36	11-12	11-12	11-12	11-12	11-12	11-12	11-12	11-12
37	11-12	11-12	11-12	11-12	11-12	11-12	11-12	11-12
38	11-12	11-12	11-12	11-12	11-12	11-12	11-12	11-12
39	11-12	11-12	11-12	11-12	11-12	11-12	11-12	11-12
40	11-12	11-12	11-12	11-12	11-12	11-12	11-12	11-12
41	13-15	11-12	11-12	11-12	11-12	11-12	11-12	11-12
42	13-15	13-15	13-15	13-15	13-15	13-15	11-12	11-12
43	13-15	13-15	13-15	13-15	13-15	13-15	13-15	13-15
44	13-15	13-15	13-15	13-15	13-15	13-15	13-15	13-15
45	13-15	13-15	13-15	13-15	13-15	13-15	13-15	13-15
46	13-15	13-15	13-15	13-15	13-15	13-15	13-15	13-15
47	13-15	13-15	13-15	13-15	13-15	13-15	13-15	13-15
48	16	16	16	16	13-15	13-15	13-15	13-15
49	16	16	16	16	16	16	16	16
50	16	16	16	16	16	16	16	16

TABLE 2 CONTINUED

Number of sentences in sample

	25	26	27	28	29	30	31	32
0	1	1	1	1	1	1	1	1
1	1	1	1	1	1	1	1	1
2	1	1	1	1	1	1	1	1
3	1	1	1	1	1	1	1	1
4	1	1	1	1	1	1	1	1
5	1	1	1	1	1	1	1	1
6	2	2	2	2	2	2	1	1
7	2	2	2	2	2	2	2	2
8	2	2	2	2	2	2	2	2
9	3	3	3	3	2	2	2	2
10	3	3	3	3	3	3	3	3
11	3	3	3	3	3	3	3	3
12	3	3	3	3	3	3	3	3
13	4	4	3	3	3	3	3	3
14	4	4	4	4	4	4	4	4
15	4	4	4	4	4	4	4	4
16	4	4	4	4	4	4	4	4
17	4	4	4	4	4	4	4	4
18	4	4	4	4	4	4	4	4
19	5-6	5-6	5-6	5-6	5-6	5-6	5-6	5-6
20	5-6	5-6	5-6	5-6	5-6	5-6	5-6	5-6
21	5-6	5-6	5-6	5-6	5-6	5-6	5-6	5-6
22	5-6	5-6	5-6	5-6	5-6	5-6	5-6	5-6
23	5-6	5-6	5-6	5-6	5-6	5-6	5-6	5-6
24	7-8	7-8	7-8	7-8	7-8	7-8	7-8	5-6
25	7-8	7-8	7-8	7-8	7-8	7-8	7-8	7-8
26	7-8	7-8	7-8	7-8	7-8	7-8	7-8	7-8
27	7-8	7-8	7-8	7-8	7-8	7-8	7-8	7-8
28	7-8	7-8	7-8	7-8	7-8	7-8	7-8	7-8
29	7-8	7-8	7-8	7-8	7-8	7-8	7-8	7-8
30	9-10	9-10	9-10	7-8	7-8	7-8	7-8	7-8
31	9-10	9-10	9-10	9-10	9-10	9-10	9-10	9-10
32	9-10	9-10	9-10	9-10	9-10	9-10	9-10	9-10
33	9-10	9-10	9-10	9-10	9-10	9-10	9-10	9-10
34	9-10	9-10	9-10	9-10	9-10	9-10	9-10	9-10
35	9-10	9-10	9-10	9-10	9-10	9-10	9-10	9-10
36	9-10	9-10	9-10	9-10	9-10	9-10	9-10	9-10
37	11-12	11-12	11-12	11-12	11-12	11-12	11-12	11-12
38	11-12	11-12	11-12	11-12	11-12	11-12	11-12	11-12
39	11-12	11-12	11-12	11-12	11-12	11-12	11-12	11-12
40	11-12	11-12	11-12	11-12	11-12	11-12	11-12	11-12
41	11-12	11-12	11-12	11-12	11-12	11-12	11-12	11-12
42	11-12	11-12	11-12	11-12	11-12	11-12	11-12	11-12
43	13-15	13-15	13-15	13-15	13-15	13-15	13-15	13-15
44	13-15	13-15	13-15	13-15	13-15	13-15	13-15	13-15
45	13-15	13-15	13-15	13-15	13-15	13-15	13-15	13-15
46	13-15	13-15	13-15	13-15	13-15	13-15	13-15	13-15
47	13-15	13-15	13-15	13-15	13-15	13-15	13-15	13-15
48	13-15	13-15	13-15	13-15	13-15	13-15	13-15	13-15
49	16	16	16	16	13-15	13-15	13-15	13-15
50	16	16	16	16	16	16	16	16

Number of unfamiliar words in sample

TABLE 2 CONTINUED

Number of sentences in sample

Number of unfamiliar words in sample	33	34	35	36	37	38
0	1	1	1	1	1	1
1	1	1	1	1	1	1
2	1	1	1	1	1	1
3	1	1	1	1	1	1
4	1	1	1	1	1	1
5	1	1	1	1	1	1
6	1	1	1	1	1	1
7	2	2	2	2	2	2
8	2	2	2	2	2	2
9	2	2	2	2	2	2
10	3	3	3	3	3	3
11	3	3	3	3	3	3
12	3	3	3	3	3	3
13	3	3	3	3	3	3
14	4	4	4	4	4	4
15	4	4	4	4	4	4
16	4	4	4	4	4	4
17	4	4	4	4	4	4
18	4	4	4	4	4	4
19	5-6	5-6	5-6	4	4	4
20	5-6	5-6	5-6	5-6	5-6	5-6
21	5-6	5-6	5-6	5-6	5-6	5-6
22	5-6	5-6	5-6	5-6	5-6	5-6
23	5-6	5-6	5-6	5-6	5-6	5-6
24	5-6	5-6	5-6	5-6	5-6	5-6
25	7-8	7-8	7-8	7-8	7-8	7-8
26	7-8	7-8	7-8	7-8	7-8	7-8
27	7-8	7-8	7-8	7-8	7-8	7-8
28	7-8	7-8	7-8	7-8	7-8	7-8
29	7-8	7-8	7-8	7-8	7-8	7-8
30	7-8	7-8	7-8	7-8	7-8	7-8
31	9-10	9-10	9-10	9-10	9-10	9-10
32	9-10	9-10	9-10	9-10	9-10	9-10
33	9-10	9-10	9-10	9-10	9-10	9-10
34	9-10	9-10	9-10	9-10	9-10	9-10
35	9-10	9-10	9-10	9-10	9-10	9-10
36	9-10	9-10	9-10	9-10	9-10	9-10
37	11-12	11-12	11-12	11-12	11-12	9-10
38	11-12	11-12	11-12	11-12	11-12	11-12
39	11-12	11-12	11-12	11-12	11-12	11-12
40	11-12	11-12	11-12	11-12	11-12	11-12
41	11-12	11-12	11-12	11-12	11-12	11-12
42	11-12	11-12	11-12	11-12	11-12	11-12
43	11-12	11-12	11-12	11-12	11-12	11-12
44	13-15	13-15	13-15	13-15	13-15	13-15
45	13-15	13-15	13-15	13-15	13-15	13-15
46	13-15	13-15	13-15	13-15	13-15	13-15
47	13-15	13-15	13-15	13-15	13-15	13-15
48	13-15	13-15	13-15	13-15	13-15	13-15
49	13-15	13-15	13-15	13-15	13-15	13-15
50	16	16	16	16	16	16

TABLE 2 CONTINUED

Number of sentences in sample

	39	40	41	42	43	44
0	1	1	1	1	1	1
1	1	1	1	1	1	1
2	1	1	1	1	1	1
3	1	1	1	1	1	1
4	1	1	1	1	1	1
5	1	1	1	1	1	1
6	1	1	1	1	1	1
7	2	2	2	2	2	2
8	2	2	2	2	2	2
9	2	2	2	2	2	2
10	3	3	3	3	3	3
11	3	3	3	3	3	3
12	3	3	3	3	3	3
13	3	3	3	3	3	3
14	4	4	3	3	3	3
15	4	4	4	4	4	4
16	4	4	4	4	4	4
17	4	4	4	4	4	4
18	4	4	4	4	4	4
19	4	4	4	4	4	4
20	5-6	5-6	5-6	5-6	5-6	5-6
21	5-6	5-6	5-6	5-6	5-6	5-6
22	5-6	5-6	5-6	5-6	5-6	5-6
23	5-6	5-6	5-6	5-6	5-6	5-6
24	5-6	5-6	5-6	5-6	5-6	5-6
25	7-8	7-8	7-8	7-8	7-8	7-8
26	7-8	7-8	7-8	7-8	7-8	7-8
27	7-8	7-8	7-8	7-8	7-8	7-8
28	7-8	7-8	7-8	7-8	7-8	7-8
29	7-8	7-8	7-8	7-8	7-8	7-8
30	7-8	7-8	7-8	7-8	7-8	7-8
31	9-10	9-10	9-10	9-10	9-10	9-10
32	9-10	9-10	9-10	9-10	9-10	9-10
33	9-10	9-10	9-10	9-10	9-10	9-10
34	9-10	9-10	9-10	9-10	9-10	9-10
35	9-10	9-10	9-10	9-10	9-10	9-10
36	9-10	9-10	9-10	9-10	9-10	9-10
37	9-10	9-10	9-10	9-10	9-10	9-10
38	11-12	11-12	11-12	11-12	11-12	11-12
39	11-12	11-12	11-12	11-12	11-12	11-12
40	11-12	11-12	11-12	11-12	11-12	11-12
41	11-12	11-12	11-12	11-12	11-12	11-12
42	11-12	11-12	11-12	11-12	11-12	11-12
43	11-12	11-12	11-12	11-12	11-12	11-12
44	13-15	13-15	13-15	13-15	13-15	13-15
45	13-15	13-15	13-15	13-15	13-15	13-15
46	13-15	13-15	13-15	13-15	13-15	13-15
47	13-15	13-15	13-15	13-15	13-15	13-15
48	13-15	13-15	13-15	13-15	13-15	13-15
49	13-15	13-15	13-15	13-15	13-15	13-15
50	16	16	16	16	16	16

Number of unfamiliar words in sample

TABLE 2 CONTINUED

Number of sentences in sample

	45	46	47	48	49	50
0	1	1	1	1	1	1
1	1	1	1	1	1	1
2	1	1	1	1	1	1
3	1	1	1	1	1	1
4	1	1	1	1	1	1
5	1	1	1	1	1	1
6	1	1	1	1	1	1
7	2	2	2	2	2	2
8	2	2	2	2	2	2
9	2	2	2	2	2	2
10	3	3	2	2	2	2
11	3	3	3	3	3	3
12	3	3	3	3	3	3
13	3	3	3	3	3	3
14	3	3	3	3	3	3
15	4	4	4	4	4	4
16	4	4	4	4	4	4
17	4	4	4	4	4	4
18	4	4	4	4	4	4
19	4	4	4	4	4	4
20	5-6	5-6	5-6	5-6	5-6	5-6
21	5-6	5-6	5-6	5-6	5-6	5-6
22	5-6	5-6	5-6	5-6	5-6	5-6
23	5-6	5-6	5-6	5-6	5-6	5-6
24	5-6	5-6	5-6	5-6	5-6	5-6
25	7-8	7-8	7-8	7-8	7-8	7-8
26	7-8	7-8	7-8	7-8	7-8	7-8
27	7-8	7-8	7-8	7-8	7-8	7-8
28	7-8	7-8	7-8	7-8	7-8	7-8
29	7-8	7-8	7-8	7-8	7-8	7-8
30	7-8	7-8	7-8	7-8	7-8	7-8
31	7-8	7-8	7-8	7-8	7-8	7-8
32	9-10	9-10	9-10	9-10	9-10	9-10
33	9-10	9-10	9-10	9-10	9-10	9-10
34	9-10	9-10	9-10	9-10	9-10	9-10
35	9-10	9-10	9-10	9-10	9-10	9-10
36	9-10	9-10	9-10	9-10	9-10	9-10
37	9-10	9-10	9-10	9-10	9-10	9-10
38	11-12	11-12	11-12	11-12	11-12	11-12
39	11-12	11-12	11-12	11-12	11-12	11-12
40	11-12	11-12	11-12	11-12	11-12	11-12
41	11-12	11-12	11-12	11-12	11-12	11-12
42	11-12	11-12	11-12	11-12	11-12	11-12
43	11-12	11-12	11-12	11-12	11-12	11-12
44	13-15	13-15	13-15	13-15	13-15	13-15
45	13-15	13-15	13-15	13-15	13-15	13-15
46	13-15	13-15	13-15	13-15	13-15	13-15
47	13-15	13-15	13-15	13-15	13-15	13-15
48	13-15	13-15	13-15	13-15	13-15	13-15
49	13-15	13-15	13-15	13-15	13-15	13-15
50	16	16	13-15	13-15	13-15	13-15

Number of unfamiliar words in sample

APPENDIX: EXAMPLES OF TEXT FROM WIDELY KNOWN BOOKS, NEWSPAPERS AND MAGAZINES

To clarify the scoring and to give the user a sense of what the various readability scores mean, we present excerpts from widely read books, newspapers and magazines. They illustrate the readability levels—from grade 1 to college graduate levels—and help the user gain a "feel" for the various readability levels.

All but the first excerpt have 100 words, and report the unfamiliar words (underlined), the number of sentences and the cloze and reading level scores.

Reading Level 1

One morning Toad sat in bed.
"I have many things to do," he said.
"I will write them all down on a list so that I can remember them."
Toad wrote on a piece of paper: A list of things to do today.
Then he wrote:
Wake up.
"I have done that," said Toad, and he crossed it out:

From: *Frog and Toad Together*

Readability Data
Number of Words in Sample 60
Number of Whole Sentences 6
Number of Unfamiliar Words 0
Number of Sentences
Per 100 Words* 10
Number of Unfamiliar Words
Per 100 Words* 0
Cloze Score 57
Reading Level 1

*For samples shorter than 100 words, see page 2.

Reading Level 2

"You said you didn't want it," said <u>Thelma</u>. "And anyhow, I don't want to sell it now."
"Why not?" said <u>Frances</u>.
"Well," said Thelma, "it is a very good tea set. It is <u>plastic</u> that does not break.
It has pretty red flowers on it.
It has all the cups and saucers.
It has the sugar bowl and the cream pitcher and the teapot.
It is almost new, and I think it cost a lot of money."
"I have two dollars and seventeen cents," said Frances.
"That's a lot of money."
"I don't know," said Thelma.
"If I sell you ...."

From: *A Bargain for Frances*

Readability Data
Number of Words in Sample 100
Number of Whole Sentences 12
Number of Unfamiliar Words 3
Cloze Score 55
Reading Level 2

Reading Level 3

Once upon a time a very small witch was walking in the woods. The cold wind was blowing the dry leaves all around her. The little witch was <u>frantically</u> searching for a house for the winter. She could not find one. Suddenly a piece of orange paper, <u>blown</u> by the wind, landed at her feet. She picked it up.
The little witch looked <u>closely</u> at the paper and then she said, "I shall make myself a little house from this piece of orange paper."
She folded the paper in half. Then she took her scissors (she always carried a pair ....

From: *Highlights for Children*

Readability Data
Number of Words in Sample 100
Number of Whole Sentences 8
Number of Unfamiliar Words 3
Cloze Score 53
Reading Level 3

Reading Level 4

Seals are wonderful <u>divers</u>. Some seals can dive several hundred feet below the surface. On deep dives, they can stay underwater up to 40 minutes without surfacing to breathe. They have special <u>features</u> to help save <u>oxygen</u> on such dives. When seals dive, they stop breathing. For very deep dives, their blood flows to everything except <u>critical</u> organs stops or slows. Seals can also slow their heart rates, sometimes to one-tenth the rates at the surface.

You may wonder how seals <u>avoid</u> the *bends* on deep dives. The bends are a painful <u>condition</u>. They are caused when <u>nitrogen</u> <u>dissolves</u> in ....

From: *The Harp Seal*

Readability Data

Number of Words in Sample	100
Number of Whole Sentences	9
Number of Unfamiliar Words	8
Cloze Score	49
Reading Level	4

Reading Level 5-6

Eskimos of <u>Alaska's</u> <u>Arctic</u> north coast have hunted whales for <u>centuries</u>.

<u>Survival</u> has depended on killing the 60-foot-long bowhead whales that swim from the <u>Bering</u> Sea to the ice-<u>clogged</u> <u>Beaufort</u> Sea each Spring. The Eskimos' <u>entire</u> way of life has been centered around the hunt.

But now that way of life is being <u>threatened</u> by America's need for oil, say many Eskimos who hunt the whales.

Huge amounts of oil may be beneath the Beaufort Sea. And oil companies want to begin drilling this spring.

However, many Eskimos say <u>severe</u> storms and ice <u>conditions</u> make drilling dangerous ....

From: *My Weekly Reader*, Edition 6

Readability Data

Number of Words in Sample	100
Number of Whole Sentences	6
Number of Unfamiliar Words	11
Cloze Score	42
Reading Level	5-6

Reading Level 7-8

Why is it that as soon as "<u>Jingle</u> Bells" starts playing on the radio, <u>otherwise</u>-<u>sane</u> people are <u>driven</u> to <u>extremes</u> to <u>create</u> the <u>Perfect</u> Christmas? Take the case of <u>Maureen</u> <u>McFadden</u>, a *Woman's Day* <u>editor</u>, who decided to <u>decorate</u> her tree with homemade <u>gingerbread</u> <u>ornaments</u>. "I started late in the evening," she <u>recalled</u>. "And then I knocked the <u>molasses</u> jar on the floor." It was downhill from there. Her cat—long-haired, of course—sat in the <u>molasses</u> pool. "And when I <u>yelped</u>, he ran down the hall into my bedroom <u>spewing</u> <u>molasses</u> everywhere." Still, after she washed the ....

From: *Woman's Day*

Readability Data

Number of Words in Sample	100
Number of Whole Sentences	7
Number of Unfamiliar Words	19
Cloze Score	36
Reading Level	7-8

Reading Level 9-10

The <u>controversy</u> over the <u>laser</u>-armed <u>satellite</u> boils down to two related questions: Will it be <u>technically</u> <u>effective</u>? And should the United States make a <u>massive</u> <u>effort</u> to <u>deploy</u> it?

To its <u>backers</u>, the <u>laser</u> seems the <u>perfect</u> weapon. Traveling in a straight line at <u>186,000</u> miles <u>per</u> second, a <u>laser</u> beam is tens of thousands of times as fast as any bullet or rocket. It could strike its <u>target</u> with a power of many <u>watts</u> <u>per</u> square inch. The <u>resulting</u> heat, <u>combined</u> with a <u>mechanical</u> shock wave <u>created</u> by recoil as surface <u>layers</u> were blasted away, would quickly melt ....

From: *Discover*

Readability Data

Number of Words in Sample	100
Number of Whole Sentences	5
Number of Unfamiliar Words	23
Cloze Score	28
Reading Level	9-10

Reading Level 11-12

The latest finding is a refinement of evidence presented last summer by audio expert James Barger — who testified there was a 50 percent probability that four shots were recorded on the tape. Barger had recorded test firings at various points in the Dealey Plaza, then compared them with the motorcycle recording. The greatest similarity was produced by two shots from the book depository, one from the knoll and another from the depository. But Barger did not draw firm conclusions because he could not pinpoint the policeman's motorcycle; his estimate could have been 18 feet off in any direction. Weiss, whose ....

From: *Newsweek*

Readability Data

Number of Words in Sample	100
Number of Whole Sentences	4
Number of Unfamiliar Words	23
Cloze Score	25
Reading Level	11-12

Reading Level 13-15

Until the 1940's, there were no specific psychiatric drugs. Bromides, barbiturates, and opiates were known to sedate disturbed patients but did not reverse the symptoms of severe mental illnesses such as the schizophrenias or manic-depressive psychoses. They did ameliorate anxiety, but only at the cost of fogging the minds of the recipients, who had to decide between being unhappy and being intoxicated. In the 1950's, the first specific drug appeared: chlorpromazine (trade name Thorazine). It was synthesized when an antihistamine chemical relative was found to sedate surgical patients. However, clinical observations showed that this drug did much more than simply ....

From: *Psychology Today*

Readability Data

Number of Words in Sample	100
Number of Whole Sentences	5
Number of Unfamiliar Words	35
Cloze Score	17
Reading Level	13-15

Reading Level 16+

Further support for the view that educational expansion would reduce inequalities was derived from the dualistic nature of developing societies. The economic structures of developing societies were said to consist of two sectors: a traditional sector that uses little capital, is relatively unproductive, does not require an educated labor force, and places a great emphasis on subsistence farming, small workshops and small commercial enterprises; and a modern sector that uses advanced technology and capital, is far more productive, and requires a labor force with at least some schooling. Expanding the educational system would qualify more workers for jobs where demands ....

From: *Harvard Educational Review*

Readability Data

Number of Words in Sample	100
Number of Whole Sentences	2
Number of Unfamiliar Words	37
Cloze Score	-6
Reading Level	16+